Philosophical Essays
on Dance

Philosophical Essays on Dance

With Responses from Choreographers, Critics and Dancers

Based on a conference at the AMERICAN DANCE FESTIVAL

Edited by
GORDON FANCHER
and GERALD MYERS

ISBN 0-87127-126-5

Library of Congress Catalog Card Number 81-67061
Printed in the United States of America

Dance Horizons, 1801 East 26th Street, Brooklyn, N.Y. 11229

Cover and interior design by Bert Waggott

Contents

THE PAPERS AND DISCUSSIONS of this book are revised versions of what were presented publicly in the summer of 1979 at the American Dance Festival on the campus of Duke University in Durham, North Carolina. The papers and discussions were delivered as a series of public events under the title "Dance Town Hall." The original events and their developments into this book were sponsored and supported by the American Dance Festival. The Rockefeller Foundation and the North Carolina Humanities Committee provided the generous funding that was required for both "Dance Town Hall" and the development of this book.

Participants

Noël Carroll:	Assistant Professor of Cinema Studies, New York University
Marshall Cohen:	Executive Officer, Philosophy Department, The Graduate Center, City University of New York
Laura Dean:	Choreographer, *Laura Dean Dancers*, New York City
Senta Driver:	Choreographer, *Harry*, New York City
Gordon Fancher:	Lecturer in Philosophy, Hunter College
Maxine Greene:	Professor of Aesthetics and Education, Columbia University
Lucas Hoving:	former Principal Dancer, *José Limón Dance Company*, New York
Deborah Jowitt:	Dance Critic, *The Village Voice*
Anna Kisselgoff:	Dance Critic, *The New York Times*
Gerald Myers:	Professor of Philosophy, City University of New York
Marcia Siegel:	Dance Critic and author of *At the Vanishing Point, Watching the Dance Go By*, and *The Shapes of Change*
Thomas Wartenberg:	Assistant Professor of Philosophy, Duke University
Paul Ziff:	Kenan Professor of Philosophy, University of North Carolina, Chapel Hill

Introduction to the Essays

by Gordon Fancher

I T I S A R A R E E V E N T when artists, critics and philosophers gather to discuss an art form. It is even more unusual when the art form discussed is dance.

Such an event took place in the summer of 1979, when the American Dance Festival invited six philosophers to present papers on dance during the Festival. Following each paper was a discussion led by a panel of both choreographers and critics. Those six philosophical essays and the discussions which followed make up this collection.

As some of the exchanges in the discussions indicate, the results were not always harmonious. There can be a real tension among practitioners of an art, those who criticize and write histories about an art, and those who philosophize about an art. Each is involved in a very different kind of activity. Nevertheless the initiators of the

1

project believed something valuable could be gained by bringing together dancers and commentators. The development of historical, critical and philosophical studies have contributed substantially to the development of art forms. Clearly the arts have benefited from exchanges between the culture of creation and the culture of commentary.

Although dance has not gone unmentioned in philosophical literature, it has not received the attention that has been given to the other arts. Compared with the corpus of literature devoted to film, drama and painting, that devoted to dance is relatively small. The papers presented in this collection demonstrate how dance can emerge as a topic of serious philosophical and critical inquiry.

The lack of attention paid to dance in philosophy is illustrated with particular irony in Hegel's *Lectures on Fine Art.* There the irony rests in the fact that dance receives only cursory treatment as a minor art form, and yet, more than any other art form, would seem to satisfy the requirements Hegel sets down for an ideal art form. For Hegel the work of art is an outcome of man's attempt to heal the breach between spirit and an alien nature, between thought and that which is merely external. The creative purposes of the artist are imposed upon a sensuous material thereby yielding a unity of spirit and sensuous form. Art reaches its ideal in classical sculpture, which achieves a perfect fusion of spiritual and material form by presenting the Greek gods in human form. According to Hegel, the "human form is alone capable of revealing the spiritual" in a sensuous material.

But if we are to take literally the requirement of a human form, dance would seem to meet it in a way that sculpture cannot. For although the Greek sculptor gave his material a human shape, the material itself was not human but merely bronze or marble. The human body of the dancer, much more so than a sculptural representation of the human body, would seem to provide the ideal sensuous embodiment of spirit. In the dancer there is a full and complete intimacy between creative thought and bodily expression. The creative design and the art form itself are merged: the artist becomes the work of art. This would seem to be just the total fusion of spirit and matter that Hegel and many of his contemporaries sought in an art work.

Why then was it so easy for Hegel to pass over dance as an inconsequential art form? The primary reason was that the dance experienced by him and his contemporaries was inconsequential. Whereas he had access not only to the drama and sculpture of his day, but also to that of the Greeks, the dance that was available to him for theoretical consideration was limited to what was being performed and taught at the time. This brings out an important factor in the formulation of theoretical accounts of dance. Accounts of dance are far more dependent upon contemporary practice than are accounts of the other arts.

An explanation of this dependence upon contemporary practice can no doubt be given in terms of those features of dance which have prompted the assertion that dance is the most elusive of the arts. The essays of Greene, Myers and Ziff all deal directly with this claim, and the remaining essays touch on issues relevant to the truth of this claim, the understanding of and evaluation of which is certainly central to an adequate aesthetic of dance.

The reality of the dance seems to lie completely in its coming to be and passing away before us. As Merce Cunningham has said, the dance is like water running through our fingers. Often the only record of the work is in the memory of the choreographer and embedded in the dancers' bodies. This makes it difficult to pin down the work. With a play we can consult the script before and after a performance. Likewise with music we can consult the score. Notational systems have been devised for dance, but whether one sees dance works as elusive will depend on one's estimation of the success of these notational systems in articulating the nuances of performance that are essential to the work.

Of course, any work in the performing arts is elusive, in that no textual account can anticipate all the nuances and subtleties that arise at the level of performance. We would not expect any notation to capture the coloring of a singer's voice or the pecularity of an actor's gesture. But the nuances that emerge in performance have a role in fixing the identity of dance works that they do not have in fixing the identity of dramatic and musical works. The playwright and composer complete their work with the setting of the verbal text or musical score. The choreographer, on the other hand, does not conclude his work with a text that is used by others as a basis for performance. Instead he carries his creative design through to the performance, setting his work on the dancers themselves. Hence, nuances of performance emerge in the very setting of the work.

Since the choreographer's control over his work extends to the

3

level of performance, what he creates will necessarily involve the elusiveness that we associate with performance. Such elusiveness, of course, emerges in the other performing arts but it does not play a central role in fixing the identity of individual works. Because the choreographer's work is so intimately related to the final performance he is less like the dramatist or composer and more like the sculptor or painter in enjoying a certain kind of control over his work. But since what he is controlling is human movement and performance and not words, sounds, pigment or stone, there is an elusiveness at the center of his work.

MAXINE GREENE in her essay "Aesthetic Education and Dance" appropriately began the series of papers with the question of whether we can talk about dance at all. Is there something about the nature of dance that eludes our verbal accounts of it? Whereas in literary art, critical conceptualization and discussion are thought essential to a full understanding of the art, in dance these are often thought not only unnecessary but a direct interference with our experience of the art. In literary art, and in some modern forms of painting and music, the experience of the art is considered greatly enriched by being guided by critical concepts of the work. In dance this sort of critical guidance is often thought to detract from the immediacy with which the dance communicates.

Maxine Greene is not satisfied with this non-verbal approach to dance and sees a dance literacy as essential to any attempt at locating dance in the domain of the arts. She argues for a literacy attained through what she calls aesthetic education. Aesthetic education involves cultivating a mode of apprehension which differs from the ways people attend to activities outside the context of art. The perspective of this aesthetic mode enables us to see dance as more than a form of entertainment or a social practice. It modifies our practical concerns and enables us to see dance as an object in aesthetic space.

GERALD MYERS in his paper "Do You See What the Critic Sees?" takes up several closely-related problems concerning the critical response to dance. Where are we to locate those things in dance which move us? Are they qualities of the performance itself or conditions of our own response? In characterizing a movement as "flowing," are we responding to an actual quality in the movement,

4

or is our characterization grounded merely in our subjective response?

Because of the ephemeral nature of dance the dance critic appears to be in a peculiar position. After the performance, no text or record is left behind and, as one leading dance critic has put it, we seem to be left with only the afterimages of a performance. But Myers urges us to resist the temptation to think of the afterimage as the proper subject matter of dance criticism. Myers feels that to succumb to this temptation has unfortunate consequences. It encourages the critic to defend criticism on the grounds that the issue is a subjective one and the aim is merely to faithfully report on what remains as memory images. Myers does not want critical discussion to retreat from such statements as, "Her dancing was fluid," to "It seemed to me that her dancing was fluid." The retreated-to claim is, of course, less open to challenge, but it directs our attention away from the art work and towards our response to the art work.

This could result in critical disagreements becoming merely questions of whether our memory images match those of the critic. This is highly unsatisfactory since, for Myers, the obvious question is whether our images and the critic's images accurately reflect the true nature of the performance. Toward the end of the paper he reminds us of what is at stake:

> Subjectivism tends to shift the focus from performance to critic, from dancer to critic. It creates a schism between art and criticism. . . . It divides what the critic sees, not merely from what we see, but also from what the dancer does.

Myers wants to offer an exposition of dance and criticism in which "the performance, not the memory of it, is the subject of dance criticism." For him the central notion in the appreciation and evaluation of any dance performance is the "quality of movement." In the art of dance "movement quality" is the basic item of aesthetic appreciation, as the quality of the voice is in singing, the quality of the brush-stroke in painting, and so on. Movement quality is what marks the difference between two dancers executing identical movements. One dancer may be praised because his movement is more "fluid" than the other's. Myers insists the word "fluid" refers to the quality of the dancer's movement, not to the viewer's subjective response.

If we allow that qualities of movement are objective features of the dancer's movements, we require an explanation for why some people fail to see them or why critics can be in dispute over their presence. How can these objective features become so extraordinarily elusive? Such elusiveness might tempt us to return to a subjectivist account of their status as existing only in the eye of the beholder. Eschewing the subjectivist alternative, Myers offers an explanation for why movement qualities can be so easily overlooked and the object of disagreement. The explanation is given in terms of our seeing being guided by certain preconceptions. We come to see what the critic sees by sharing certain of his preconceptions about what to look for and how to recognize it.

In the discussion following Myers' paper, some choreographers and critics objected to the notion that the quality of a particular dance movement could be accurately reported in objective statements. This objection was linked to the feeling that dance could not be captured within an imposed conceptual framework, that it eluded and resisted analysis. Marcia Siegel expressed this feeling well in her reluctance to accept "an intellectual framework that is perhaps more definite and more positive and more graspable' than the experience itself."

PAUL ZIFF, in his paper "About the Appreciation of Dance," addresses certain problems central to the appreciation and evaluation of dance. Ziff organizes his paper around the issue of whether dance can be seen as language. Though it is possible to find syntactic and semantic structures in dance, Ziff does not feel these are sufficient to qualify dance as a language. In the course of separating out the syntactical features of dance, Ziff discusses several interesting philosophical questions. Can we draw the line between what is dance and what isn't? Initially we might feel there ought to be a way of doing this. Suppose we have absolute stillness on the stage, no changes in movement, lighting or set. Or suppose a performance is given in complete darkness so no movement is seen. Could we call these dances? Ziff finds no way for deciding such a question and thinks it is perhaps not crucial that we do so. In the discussion following the paper, Senta Driver found this decision to be a wise one, since drawing a line between what is dance and what isn't only acts as a challenge for choreographers to create a non-dance.

Ziff feels there is a problem at the syntactical level that poses enormous difficulties for the appreciation and evaluation of dance. It is the problem of perspective. The configurations the dancers create in the context of lighting, sound and backdrop will look different according to the point from which the dance is viewed. There will be a radical difference, for example, in a view from below the action and a view from overhead. A viewer in one part of the theater will be seeing something different from what a viewer in another part sees.

No doubt, such facts are well known to dance-goers, but they probably have not reflected on the uniqueness of this problem of perspective as it arises in theater dance. You can view a painting or sculpture from a number of different points, and each of these points is accessible to every viewer. But the dance viewer cannot gain a new perspective on the same movement by moving from one part of the theater to another. By the time the dance viewer has changed his perspective the dance movement has also changed. Attending to the full visual reality of the configuration of movement would seem to require a godlike awareness. In contrast, a musical performance, if the hall has been designed correctly, does allow the listeners to share a single perspective. In a properly-designed hall one seat is as good as another for hearing everything there is to be heard. Dance viewers can compensate for these differences in viewpoint by a familiarity with the traditions and conventions of dance. Background knowledge enables viewers to transcend, to some extent at least, their differences in visual experience. Yet the interesting fact remains that this compensation is a requirement uniquely made of dance audiences.

The other major problem at the syntactical level, according to Ziff, is the difficulty of finding a basis for identifying an individual dance work. In drama we can identify a play on the basis of a script. Although choreographers make use of notational systems, Ziff feels there is no notational system in use that approaches the explicitness we get in a script.

Some dance notators would argue that Ziff is wrong about this, that there are notational devices that can pin down the dance work to the same extent a script can pin down a play. At the other extreme, some would claim Ziff has made the inadequacy of dance notation merely a factual matter. According to this view, it is a matter of principle or logic that notational devices are incapable of capturing the reality of a dance work. Dance works are understood as unique in their transcendence of any symbolic accounts of them.

When we consider the semantic level of dance, according to Ziff, it becomes most obvious that dance is not a language. Configurations of movement simply do not yield anything corresponding to the straightforward propositional meanings of statements. Certain pantomime movements can be translated into statements, but obviously much of dance movement is not of this sort. If the dancer's movements were really part of a language, then "we should be able to say what they mean, and if we can't say what they mean, then something is wrong here." What is wrong, according to Ziff, is our unfortunate tendency to think of dance as a language.

Ziff goes on to say that although dance movement does not have linguistic meaning, it can be said to have remarkable expressive value. We have little difficulty in recognizing expressive characteristics either in everyday life or in dance movement. Yet we are not able to provide an analysis of why certain physiognomic characteristics strike us as awesome or sad. The only reason we see certain looks and movements as expressive may be that "human beings are innately structured to respond" in this way. The lack of such an analysis, far from making dance criticism impossible, makes it essential. We need critics who are sensitive in knowing what to look for. Such critics can suggest new ways of seeing things we have failed to notice. Also, a thorough familiarity with the dance can enable a critic to aid us in overcoming the problem of visual perspective.

One might wonder how human dance movement could fail to be expressive. Yet one of the avowed aims of a number of post-modern choreographers has been to rid movements of any expressive quality. In his paper "Post-Modern Dance and Expression," NOËL CARROLL attempts to evaluate this commitment on the part of a number of post-modern choreographers and dancers to achieve movement that does not express any human emotion or feeling. In particular he takes a close look at Yvonne Rainer's *Trio A*, a work which appears to subvert all the usual characteristics attributed to dance, including the expression of human emotion.

In order to evaluate such avant-garde works, Carroll finds it necessary to distinguish several different senses in which a dance might be expressive. The usual sense and what Carroll calls the narrowest sense is the expression of human feelings such as joy, anguish, terror and ambivalence. For example, when the dancer's movements and the total context convey inner turmoil, we can say "the movement metaphorically has the quality of inner turmoil." In such works as *Trio A* Carroll believes avant-garde choreographers have indeed "drained expression from their choreography in the narrowest sense of expression, that is, the expression of feelings."

Carroll suggests there is a "broad sense" in which dance movements are expressive; they can express or communicate ideas. A dance, inevitably by having the place it has in the history of dance tradition, necessarily reflects choreographic choices made *vis-à-vis* those traditions. The choreographic choices can show an endorsement of prevailing techniques and presuppositions, or it can indicate a rejection. The choreography of *Trio A* is self-consciously polemical against the balletic and modern tradition. Rainer is saying "no" to the inclusion of expressive quality in choreography. In denying expression a place in her choreography, she is on another level expressing this negation. It is difficult to imagine how any dance could fail to be expressive insofar as it cannot avoid expressing its position within its historical context.

Carroll goes on to make the point that, once we locate the dance's expression with respect to its historical setting, we can also see it as expressing certain broad anthropomorphic qualities. Avant-garde dances that set themselves against what is "emotive" and "impassioned" can thereby be seen as "cool," "objective," "factual." Thus Carroll concludes that Rainer and other avant-garde choreographers, in pursuing their intention to eradicate expression in the narrowest sense, introduced expressive qualities at other levels.

In the discussion which followed Carroll's paper, Paul Ziff suggested that if the choreographer wished to avoid expressing not only feelings, but also anything from an historical context, then he should simply not show his work. Total non-expression in dance would require finding a correlation to the painter who achieves non-expression in his work by immediately burning it upon completion.

Some interesting questions arose in the discussion concerning how the intentions of performers enter into the expressive quality of a dance. It was suggested that the mere presence of a living human body in a performance generated an expressive quality. Senta Driver cited a four-hour performance in which the dancer remained completely still. She considered that to be an example of expressive movement, not the least reason being that "the performer was not dead." One might feel there is an expressiveness generated solely out of performing or making oneself available to an audience. If we can construe the expressiveness of performance to be as basic as the expression of such feelings as sadness, then Rainer and others failed to achieve non-expressive dance even in the narrowest sense. It was suggested that perhaps what Rainer really wanted was a performance of *Trio A* without performers.

The performer in a so-called non-expressive dance would seem to be faced with some interesting questions about what is or is not to be conveyed. How does one follow either explicit or implicit directions not to express anything? Does one adopt a blank stare, a studied indifference, or perhaps a look of "Don't mind me, I'm not really doing anything"? We could, however, come to associate certain looks in performance with a choreographic intention to be non-expressive.

In his paper "Is Dance Elitist?" THOMAS WARTENBERG considers the question of whether certain dance movements are elitist. The assertion that certain dance movements are elitist might be understood in several different ways:

1. Dance movements are elitist if they require a high degree of skill to execute.
2. Dance movements are elitist if they are intended to appeal only to a highly selective audience.
3. Dance movements are elitist if they are associated with a subject matter that has an elitist or aristocratic content.
4. Dance movements are elitist if they are movements characteristic of an elite or aristocratic class.
5. Dance movements are elitist if they are movements that represent what an elite class regards as ideal movements.

Wartenberg is primarily concerned with the fourth and fifth claims. Wartenberg characterizes elitism as the belief that some human beings are superior to others because they possess certain characteristics. Non-elitist or democratic views of human beings do not rank or evaluate human beings on the basis of their characteristics. The democratic view "sees all human beings as equally worthy."

One can see balletic movement as characteristic of and originating in the aristocratic courts of Europe. But it is the selection process presupposed in balletic movement that Wartenberg finds more important. He says that behind any basic vocabulary of movement, such as ballet, there is a selection process that includes certain movements and excludes others. By virtue of this selection process, any vocabulary of movement presents "an idealized version of human nature." The balletic vocabulary presents us with the aristocratic ideal of human movement. It reflects aristocratic choices about what is beautiful and what is not. In exalting certain movements, it also demeans others.

If we accept the balletic vocabulary as a standard of human movement, then, according to Wartenberg, we are endorsing the aristocratic choices reflected therein. We are allowing our standard of movement to be determined by an aristocratic or elitist view of the world.

Wartenberg thinks the early pioneers of modern dance such as Isadora Duncan and Doris Humphrey were right to reject the balletic standard of movement. In departing from the balletic vocabulary the modern dance movement allowed us "to look at all movement as an appropriate object for aesthetic appraisal." He characterizes the democratization of dance in the following way:

> And it is this openness, this sense of alternative vocabularies and differing perspectives, that is the kernel of the democratic spirit of modern dance, for it validates each individual's attempt to define for himself an authentic sense of movement, a fitting model for a truly democratic sense of life itself. No longer need we see beautiful movement as the province of a single class. Any movement may be beautiful, depending on how it fits into a choreographer's vision.

Wartenberg's charge that balletic movement is elitist should not be understood as an objection to the fact that it allows only certain movements. Any art form could be understood as elitist in the sense of excluding certain possibilities. In the discussion it was pointed out that we wouldn't want to call a style of music undemocratic because it excludes quarter-tones from the scale. Wartenberg agreed, since he was not simply saying ballet movement excluded other possibilities. He had argued that the principle of selectivity used in ballet had been determined by an elite class of people. It is in our sharing their principle of selectivity that we too become elitists.

Wartenberg's paper stimulated two kinds of questions. First, do historical and anthropological studies support the contention that the balletic ideals of grace and beauty distinctly belong to an elite class? Second, even if it is true that balletic movement is primarily associated with elitist views of movement, would it not be possible to accept the balletic standard of movement without accepting an elitist ideology? Could we follow the elitist in his ideology of movement without endorsing his politics?

Marshall Cohen suggested there might be an alternative way of approaching the social issue. Instead of shunning the balletic standard because of its aristocratic associations we might want to create a world in which everyone can achieve the balletic values of grace and beauty in a way that is not now open to them.

In his essay "Primitivism, Modernism and Dance Theory" MARSHALL COHEN skillfully delineates the problems inherent in arriving at an adequate theoretical account of dance. Cohen employs philosophical analysis in a way that is sensitive to both the historical tradition and the contemporary practice of dance. The essay is largely devoted to evaluating two influential accounts of dance, Suzanne Langer's and David Levin's. He looks at these accounts in light of two predominant ideals of modern art upon which they have drawn.

The first ideal of modern art is associated with Wagner's notion of the *Gesamtkunstwerk*. Here the ideal is to merge the most powerful resources of the various arts into a single and total work of art. Cohen notes this desire for a total and unspecialized experience in theatre has primitivist aspects. It is sometimes claimed that in primitive religion and art there is no dissociation between reality and image. A synthesis of the arts to create a singular unified experience can be seen as a way of restoring this primitive unity. It is possible to see dance as the art which best exemplifies this primitive unity and thus as uniquely qualified to draw together the various art media into a total work of art. For a number of reasons Cohen feels the *Gesamtkunstwerk* ideal cannot provide an acceptable account of dance. He concludes that "the art of dance as we know and experience it is one among the arts. It does not displace or incorporate all the other arts, not even the other theatrical arts."

Susanne Langer, like the proponents of the *Gesamtkunstwerk*, looks to primitive art for an understanding of dance. Unlike these proponents, she does not seek to recover that primitive experience in order to create a total theater experience with dance at the center. Rather she seeks to understand how what was once a mystical fusion of symbol and reality has become for us something quite different. Dance has become an object of aesthetic experience, and for her that means the dance must be something primarily visual, an image or an illusion. For Langer, to approach dance as an art is to treat it as something purely visual and not to confuse it with what is practical or real. Expressions of emotions in dance, for example, are not in fact expressions of an individual's emotions. Langer sees such expressions as merely illusory and characterizes dance as an art of illusory gesture. Cohen questions this way of thinking of dance movement and feels Langer's theory is unable to account for the minimalist works of contemporary dance that intentionally refrain from transforming physical movement into gesture.

The world image created by the dance, like the role of gesture in dance, is central to Langer's view. This image retains some of the characteristics of the original primitive experience. She describes it as an image of "interacting forces" which appear "to move the dance itself." The illusion created is one of a "conquest of gravity," a freedom from the forces that normally control the dancer's body. As Cohen points out, Langer's argument for the illusion of weightlessness contradicts the importance modern dance places on acknowledging the gravitational pull on the dancer's body. In his criticism of Langer, Cohen makes the point that "dance is not a purely visual art." Individual virtuosity has been an important part of our appreciation of dance "and this requires that we have reason to believe the image is created in a certain way." The cinematic trick that gives us Fred Astaire dancing on the wall and ceiling in *Royal Wedding* or the invisible flying wires at one time used in Romantic ballet do not provide us with the same satisfaction we experience in watching the efforts of dancers overcoming the forces that normally control their bodies and movements.

Modernism, the more recent ideal of modern art, attempts to achieve a clear separation of the individual arts — to isolate, purify and intensify that which is peculiar to each art. A number of different ideas have been associated with modernism. Cohen clarifies these ideas by distinguishing three primary concerns of modernism found in Clement Greenberg's influential account.

First, modernism can be seen as a requirement for frankness in art. A work must clearly acknowledge its physicality. It cannot be involved in creating an illusion. The artifice behind art must be removed. Deception at one time had been thought of as a virtue in art. Edmund Burke, writing in the eighteenth century, declared: "All art is as great as it deceives." Writing several years later, Carlo

Blasis, in his treatise on dancing, advised all dancers to follow the precept of Luigi Riccoboni: "Nothing is more dangerous to art than to permit the spectator to penetrate its simulation." In contrast, modernism appears in dance when the dancer sheds all pretense of being anything other than a moving human body.

The second idea of modernism Cohen elucidates is that of propriety. Each art is required to stay within the domain of its own medium and not to trespass on the domain of another. The modernist aesthetic, for example, tells the painter to be purely optical and not to be involved in telling a story, since that would be an infringement upon the domain of literature. The same sort of reasoning would require that dancers stay strictly within the domain of movement and not speak, sing or even move in a way that would serve to tell a story. Cohen points out that another requirement often invoked in the name of modernism, namely, that the other arts follow painting in becoming purely optical, demands the suspension of the propriety requirement. For dance, the requirement to be purely optical would mean deferring to sculpture any claim on the three-dimensional.

The third idea associated with modernism that Cohen distinguishes is minimalism. The minimalist demand on the art form is to exhibit only what is essential to the form. "Modernism in this sense requires that the work of art 'reveal,' or 'make present,' the defining conditions for being a work of its kind— that is to say, the minimal conditions for being a work in that medium." Minimalism in dance would aspire to making present the essentials of dance movement, while eliminating any feature of dance that did not participate in this display. The expression of feeling, the telling of a story, the response to a musical structure could all be eliminated from dance movement on this basis.

It is modernism in the form of minimalism that Cohen finds as a useful background for approaching David Levin's essay, "Balanchine's Formalism." Levin follows the example of Michael Fried in looking for the minimal conditions of the art work. In Fried's view the minimalist work reveals a contradiction; it reveals its essential characteristic as an object, but it also reveals the characteristics that are essential for overcoming its objecthood. Levin feels certain works of Balanchine succeed in revealing such a contradiction. The Balanchine dancer acknowledges the body's weight while at the same time achieving an illusion of weightlessness. The weightless opticality is implemented by removing mimetic gesture and dramatic implication from the choreography. As Cohen notes Levin ends up with a characterization of dance very close to Langer's, an illusory world free from the forces of gravity. He feels that even if we were to accept Levin's minimalist presuppositions, Levin's characterization of dance is no more convincing than Langer's.

But more importantly, Cohen also feels Levin has not given us an accurate description of Balanchine's art, and he goes into some detail in expressing his disagreement. According to Cohen, "Balanchine does not create the dance equivalent of the purely optical illusions of certain types of modernist painting and sculpture. Rather, Balanchine perpetuates classical ballet's idealization of the human body." Finally, a decisive reason for not seeing Balanchine as a minimalist is the manner in which his choreography is governed by the structure of the music. "The look of a Balanchine ballet can never be considered in abstraction from the music to which it is set and no consideration of the look of a Balanchine ballet could in itself account for the power of Balanchine's art."

As Cohen concludes both primitivism and modernism fail to generate an adequate account of dance. The immensely difficult task of providing an accurate description and an adequate theory of dance "largely remains to be done."

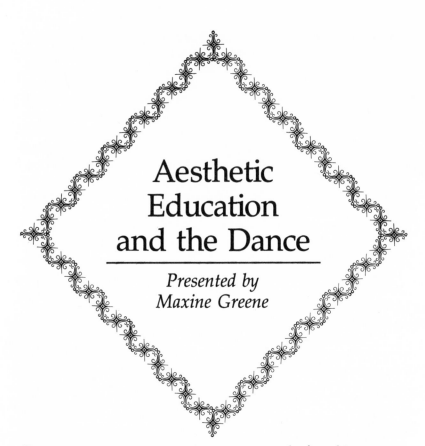

Aesthetic Education and the Dance

Presented by
Maxine Greene

THERE IS A CLEAR DELIGHT to be found in encounters with the dance. Watching bodies in motion, seeing images in lighted space, attending to figures in volatile formations, audiences respond with various degrees of acuity and enjoyment. They may be deeply moved, inspired, even awed. They may find themselves in moods of cool serenity—admiring from a distance symmetrical designs, spirals, prolongations of gesture, the sculpting of unexpected forms. What is it that affects people so, that fascinates them, that makes them come, time and time again? Is it the physical virtuosity they see displayed, the effort being exerted, the control, the discipline? Is it the emotive quality of what is being expressed? Is it the interweaving of music and movement? Or can it be the spectacle, the dramatization, the enactment of story or feeling or theme? If we can answer such questions, can we then go on and explain the existential meanings some individuals discover in experiences with dance? Can we identify the significance of dance in the landscapes of diverse lives?

On one level, it seems relatively simple. Human beings inhabit sentient bodies; each one is in the world as an embodied consciousness. Kinaesthetic responses are to be expected. Persons have the capacity to feel what they are seeing in their nerves and muscles; they can feel themselves caught up by what is happening before them, physically and organically engaged. There are the rhythms, the dynamic shapes of motion; there are pulsations that connect with the pulsations of living. The interplay of color, image, gesture, sound makes possible a total sensory involvement, whether or not there is a story or a recognizable idea. And, on another level, there is mystery, the mystery that surrounds any art form. There is something ineffable about experiences with dance, and audiences can be moved out of themselves on occasion, lured into another world. They may be, for a fleeting moment, opened to new facets of what they take to be reality. In some miraculous fashion, they may be brought in touch with themselves.

If this is what happens during dance performances, it would seem to be quite enough. I want to make the point, however, that dance pieces do not disclose themselves spontaneously. A particular mode of attending and a distinctive sending forth of energy are required if dance works are to be fully achieved—achieved as works of art. Simply to be there, to watch the performers in action on the stage, to exult over the pas de deux, to applaud the leap, to catch one's breath at the death of Giselle: all this may mean being entertained, even being enthralled. But there is always more to be discovered, more to be enjoyed. Some degree of dance literacy, attained through what can be called aesthetic education, is likely to enhance awareness as it heightens discrimination. Moreover, it is likely to empower beholders to notice much more of what there is to be noticed, to pay heed to the details, the qualitative dimensions of what they see. Their own perceived space may be illuminated in novel ways; they may respond differently to movement patterns, forms, changing styles. They may become consciously participant in what they recognize to be an aesthetic domain, consciously engaged in bringing certain dances into existence as works of art.

To speak of the art of dance, or of performances that may be realized as works of art, is to single out what are ordinarily called theatrical dances, whether narrative or abstract, intended to evoke aesthetic enjoyment in those who attend. There is no question that a particular mode of apprehension is demanded if a dance is to be perceived as art. It is a way of attending that differs from the ways in which people address themselves to disco or to other types of social dancing, to folk dancing, even to certain kinds of ceremonial dance. Dances thought of as theatrical are not intended to set audiences dancing, to create communal feeling, nor to establish a relationship with a supernatural force. Their justification is to be found in the pleasure they make possible, the visions they disclose, the perspectives they open on being physically in the world. To be literate where such dances are concerned is to be conversant with the stance, the mode of attending that permits them to *be* works of art. To be literate is to have achieved the capacity to discriminate, to pay heed to the appearances that are Martha Graham's *Night Journey* or Pilobolus or *Giselle.* It is to have achieved the ability to perceive in such a manner that what is presented on stage is actively grasped as a qualitative whole. This means something far more than a linking together, a sequence, an event occurring in time and space. A configuration must arise out of the encounter between beholders and the work: a kinetic patterning of moving bodies, lights, musical shapes, costumes, decorative designs.

Dance literacy also entails a familiarity with some of the conventions of dance. It involves an awareness that Giselle's fragmented gestures in the mad scene are gestures in an illusioned world. They are, in some sense, depictions of madness; they take on meaning in a space far removed from everyday pathologies, from the mundane. And, indeed, to be literate with respect to dance is, crucially, to be able to uncouple the experience from the useful and the ordinary and the "real." Beholders are asked to establish themselves in a psychic relation with Giselle that differs from the relation they might have with a disturbed relative, an abandoned bride, a heartbroken child down the street. They are asked to "distance" what is happening to Giselle and her prince and the village people, to move deliberately into their imaginary world. To accomplish this and at once to engage directly with what is happening demand the ability to be personally present to the dance at each moment of its performing, while "bracketing out" the familiar everyday world. What I am referring to may be described as a free act of consciousness on the part of those who behold. To grasp something by means of such an act of consciousness is to perceive it knowingly from particular standpoints, to be aware of the aspects under which what is being seen appears. Even as beholders attend to specific movement patterns and to the configurations that form and reform before their eyes, they need also to be aware of the individual characters and what they are expressing through the images they create. They need to be aware of them as they stand before consciousness at the moment of perceiving. Each beholder must experience his/her own act of perception and recognize, on some level, how such perceiving effects transformations on the stage, how the occurrences taking place are transmuted into dance. And when, by means of another act of consciousness, the same beholder allows his/her imagination to play upon what is perceived, he/she may well witness the work coming into being as a work of art.

There is more, however. There is the act of consciousness that is conceiving or conceptual understanding, something audiences tend to be wary about when it has to do with dance. This may be because the kinaesthetic and the purely sensory have been so much emphasized, and because dance makes such an immediate appeal. It is often assumed that dance (unlike poetry, say, or some kinds of painting) can speak directly and insistently to anyone willing to pay heed. Literary art, in contrast, is thought to be perfectly susceptible to cognitive treatment. Reflection upon and talk about poetry or fiction are widely believed to enrich the literary experience, to clarify rather than to detract. To a large extent, people acknowledge the same with regard to painting and music, especially in their modern forms. They are prone to agree that a Cezanne landscape, a De Kooning woman, a Debussy suite, a Stravinsky cantata are made more accessible when perception is guided by ideas. Where dance is concerned, conceptualization strikes people as extrinsic or irrelevant, except when it focuses on specific performances, or on the miracles wrought by a Baryshnikov, a Makarova, a Nureyev, a Fonteyn. When we consider the eloquent discussions of which Martha Graham, Doris Humphrey, Pauline Koner, Erick Hawkins and others have been capable, the reluctance to think cognitively about dance becomes perplexing. When, as well, we think of the increasing numbers of talented and informed dance critics, it seems odd that so many spectators find themselves to be wordless after witnessing dance. The best they can manage, more often than not, is "Fantastic!" or "Fabulous!" or "Wow!"

And audiences are unlikely to turn to critics for clues as to what to notice. Far more frequently, they look to them for prescriptions, verdicts, hints with respect to what to buy tickets for or, worse, what to like. There are those who blanch when told that something they liked especially—a Glen Tetley piece, *Orpheus, Eugene Onegin*—was unfavorably reviewed by a well-known dance critic. Instead of referring back to what they themselves perceived, readers often lament that they guessed incorrectly, that they were incompetent to judge.

One subject of an aesthetic education is to equip dance lovers with the capacity to ground their own judgments (and their recommendations) in what *they* have knowingly perceived. If they find that dance critics have different opinions, they ought to be able to understand and recognize what those critics are using as evidence and what their major premises are. Comparing what Arlene Croce calls their own "afterimages" with what they find described on the printed page, individual members of audiences ought to be enabled to discern more dimensions of their own experience with the works in question and to revise or hold to their original judgments on the basis of what they discern.

There are ways of teaching that might enable people to consult dance critics as guides to seeing and guides to articulation. Good critics, after all, *point* to details, to dimensions of dance works that might otherwise remain invisible to the ordinary viewer. They highlight particular qualities (their intensity, their vividness, their poignancy, their clarity) and indicate how formal unities are made possible, how the particulars come together (when they do) into more or less coherent wholes. If they know how to share their own informed visions, they are able to take their readers on journeys through an *Orpheus* or a *Eugene Onegin* for the sake of indicating dynamic images, moments of counterpoint, symmetrical or asymmetrical designs, diagonals, the shapes of despair and outrage and pure joy. It may take an aesthetic education to understand that such journeys have the potential of clarifying reflected-on experiences with dance pieces already seen. Deborah Jowitt says critical discussions may articulate the responses audiences have had even as they stimulate new ways of seeing. This may be true; but it seems to me an amount of dance literacy is required if the critic is to have such an effect. Marcia Siegel, in her turn, attempts to draw reader attention to the changing shapes of dance throughout history. Again, viewers may need to be educated enough to perceive shape in live performances before extending their perspectives by looking through Marcia Siegel's eyes. The resources of metaphor and image so many critics have at hand surely have the potential of enhancing perception as they increase understanding; but what they write is likely to be treated primarily as literature (if not prescription) unless more efforts are made intentionally to initiate persons into the realm of dance.

The individual who has been provided opportunities to move, to find his/her own center, to explore gesture, to sketch images in space with his/her own body, may well be in the best position to appreciate the critical dimension. As I see it, an effective aesthetic educational program ought to include such opportunities, even as it offers participants performances of various kinds. Movement exercises, improvisations, creative experiments may be valuable for their own sakes; but, in the contexts of aesthetic education, they may become one of the sources of understanding what is perceived upon the stage. Anyone who has himself or herself worked to enhance a gesture, to contract, or to extend is more likely to perceive the details of such phenomena in a performance and, at once, to experience a body-response to what is seen. Activities, explorations, image-making in closed and open spaces: all these cannot but deepen apprehension, especially if efforts are made to articulate what is happening, to seek out (when appropriate) words.

Aesthetic education, of course, moves beyond what is thought to be dance appreciation as it moves beyond movement exercises. For all the increasing sophistication of dance education today, however, for all the soaring popularity of dance, for all the connections being found between dance and kinetics, dance and therapy, much remains to be done to locate the dance properly in the domain of the arts. It seems to me that occasions ought to be provided for the assimilation of dance as an art form in the sense a Henry Moore sculpture can be assimilated, Beckett's *Waiting for Godot*, Wallace Stevens' "Sunday Morning." Again, the justification for doing this is that appreciation may be heightened, enjoyment deepened if dance is fully recognized as an art.

As in the case of any other art form, more than retinal looking (and more than physical activity) are required if dance as art is to be realized in experience. There must always be some sort of conceptual knowing about the medium being used: in the case of dance, the body in motion. There must be some degree of understanding with

21

respect to the relevant notational systems, and with respect to the symbolisms that distinguish the art form. A symbolic image expressed in words (Wallace Stevens' "blue guitar," for instance; W.H. Auden's "Irish vessel . . . emptied of its poetry"; William Carlos Williams' "old bottle, mauled by the fire") is quite different from a symbolic image in a dance—Martha Graham's lonely, white-clad figure moving into the center of the three-sided arrangement of dancers in *Primitive Mysteries;* Iago leaping on Othello's back in José Limón's *The Moor's Pavane.* The intelligences at work are different. One symbolism cannot be translated into another; yet, within the domain of the artistic-aesthetic, they are in some mysterious way akin. This perception, along with the questions any discovery in the arts summons up, seems to me to play a focal role in dance literacy. The so-called "naked eye" certainly can see what is set before it; but that "naked eye" must be clothed, must be informed, if there is to be an engagement with an aesthetic object (not simply a whirl of movement, an enactment of a tale, a display of acrobatic skill) in the domain of dance. It is not merely that the uninformed viewer cannot detect all the differences between the ethereal, artificial movements in classical ballet and the expressive use of the body in modern dance. More than likely, such a viewer cannot single out the qualitative elements, the shapes and masses and tonalities that are ordinarily obscured in the common-sense world through which everyone moves among routine and practical concerns. What is needed, I am saying, is an educated understanding, not necessarily a set of analytic skills. What is needed is a sensitivity to the qualitative and the imaginary, a recognition that dance works are in some sense privileged creations, made for aesthetic apprehension, commanding aesthetic regard.

This regard cannot be legislated, and it must always be remembered that it takes time. If persons are to see more, notice more, risk a passionate presentness at moments of enactment, we need to make it possible for them to reflect in many ways and at various intervals upon their encounters with dance and, at once, their encounters with the other arts. Even as it takes hours, perhaps days, for a work of art fully to inhabit an individual's consciousness, it takes time to recognize the sense in which the work may have altered vision, affected the pulse of living, opened unexpected perspectives on what is called the "real."

Aesthetic education, as I have been describing it, builds upon participatory experiences, perceptual experiences, particular encounters with performances. Its effort is to provoke persons to reach towards new levels of generality, at which they may conceive themselves existing in aesthetic space and discover how it may mean to enter a province of meaning that opens continually new vistas upon the world. And indeed it is important to help persons challenge the calculative, the taken-for-granted, the stereotyped, as it is important to help them overcome passivity. None of this can be assumed when we see people thronging into theaters and opera houses. Nor can it be assumed that those people—open, eager, striving for sensory awareness—will discover all they are capable of discovering, enjoy what they ache to enjoy.

The questions I originally posed are in some measure unanswerable. But I am proposing the creation of situations, many-faceted situations, within schools and outside of schools, in which persons of all tastes and orientations can be freed to explore those questions in their own fashions—and, in their moving, perceiving and imagining, find the solutions for themselves.

DISCUSSION FOLLOWING
MAXINE GREENE PRESENTATION

Panelists: Lucas Hoving, Marcia Siegel,
Gerald Myers, Maxine Greene

LUCAS HOVING: The first things that came to my mind are two of my own experiences about learning how to look, how in many cases one has to undo so many things. The José Limón Company gave a performance for the Bolshoi Ballet in Juilliard, the old Juilliard Theater, and José was dancing in the first piece. I was there and talking to them, and the whole company was absolutely dancing like a dream. José started the piece and the girls were dancing like a dream, but the audience was sort of sitting. They were not getting with it, till the boys came out with an ordinary jump . . . maybe they were a little higher that night than normally, but suddenly the energy of that whole company, of that whole surrounding, went

23

zzzzz. Everybody reacted to something that was familiar there, and you know how when dancers dance for other dancers, if things are right, they really can do it well.

I remember one other incident, during a season in Mexico City. The people in the balcony, the maids, the cooks, the working people, were especially responsive to our dancing. And those people kept coming back for certain pieces, and not the easiest pieces. I remember a specific person who came back to see Doris Humphrey's *Day on Earth*. And those were people who had never seen such dance. There was some dancing in Mexico City but I don't know how much they had seen. But it made sense to me, because—30 years ago I'm talking about—I felt that in Mexico there was a certain purity in the arts, and I liked the way the houses were painted and the murals were painted and the way people dressed. It made sense that these people understood these pieces. Okay, these two different incidents came to my mind, and I'll leave it now at that.

MARCIA SIEGEL: I thought what Maxine said goes right to the point of what I've been trying to do and what a lot of us have been trying to do as critics, and those who just came yesterday to start the critics' program will be inundated by remarks like that for the next three weeks. But I think there is a confusion and there is a dichotomy—maybe it's not clear any more, or maybe things are changing. I feel there is a real difference now between the kind of criticism you're talking about and the kind of criticism I'm trying to do, and the kind of criticism a lot of people want. People want to be told what to think. They want to be told what to like, what's good and what's bad, and newspapers, which is where at the moment most dance criticism gets written, want their critics to be that kind of an arbiter, that kind of an authority. I'm talking in a practical sense because at this stage of aesthetic literacy in dance those are essentially the only ways in which criticism can get written. I don't know of any real dance critics who have any other jobs that allow them to do criticism. Most of us have other jobs, but no one is paying me to do criticism for a life work.

That puts certain kinds of pressures on the critic, time pressures and economic pressures, from the publishers in some cases, and so on. I'm not trying to cop out of this. I'm saying, we're living in a very confusing world. The critic is between the artist and the audience, and I think most of us are very aware of that responsibility

24

and that position. It is a key position, especially in dance, where, as you all know, the audience can't hold onto it, can't go back and read it again if they didn't understand it. They must rely on their critic or somebody else to validate the work for them or explain it if they need it explained. Yet the critic can only be as responsive as possible to the art that is being done, and to the climate in which that art is taking place, and I think dance right now is in a very confused state about its own aims. I just don't know if dancers know if they're making art. I think they don't know if they have time to make art. I think they don't know what kind of art they're making or who their audience is or why they're making it. A lot of what we see—and I have been saying this for some time, and as this very long season goes on I feel it more and more—there is a lot of dance that doesn't inspire me as a critic, and I'm not surprised if it doesn't inspire the audience. And I don't think it's meant to. I think a lot of it is meant to be a product, meant to be not an art at all, meant not to have those demands. I am interested in dance as an art and in writing about it as it strikes me, in resonant ways.

GERALD MYERS: I understand Maxine Greene to be saying to dancers and critics that they are creating and discussing a kind of experience created by dance that is richer than a lot of people realize. I understand her to be saying, among other things, that such richness doesn't really emerge in the presence of a vital art work unless you understand its susceptibility to conceptual interpretation, until you know its susceptibility to a tremendous amount of articulation and conceptual formulation. I take it Lucas, in referring to some of the experiences that the José Limón Company had in touring, is appreciating that fact and saying that there are audiences who do find things maybe even the artists on the stage don't realize are there. As T. S. Eliot said about poetry, a critic can sometimes find things in a poem that the poet himself didn't realize were there. So I'd like to hear more from Lucas as to what he thinks was happening on the other side of the footlights when he was performing, what kinds of special experiences that maybe he discovered later he was creating, whether he and the audience were sharing similar experiences on special occasions. And I'd like to hear more from Marcia Siegel as to whether she agrees with Maxine Greene that you really don't unlock the richness in your experience of watching a dance until you know how to inform it with crucial and critical concepts.

25

GREENE: I think what Marcia said is of enormous significance, because it says something about our cultural plight, not just about newspapers and about criticism. I think people in education have a huge responsibility to do something so people don't go for guidance in the way you were describing. It's not something critics or artists can deal with themselves; there has to be a kind of education of educators so it becomes a kind of common effort to break that terrible hold.

HOVING: I'll pick up on the last thing you said, Jerry. I think most dancers, for the longest time in their career, don't have any concrete aim. All they want is to dance: they want to get on stage. Why they want to get on stage as opposed to just dancing for themselves, I think it's a receiving of energy. You get a sort of high. And it's not a rational thing. They have that need to do this. It's a confirmation. It's a form of receiving love. I feel I worked with several people who were very committed to very important and deep causes, including José Limón. There was a lady in Holland before that, and these people were all very deeply committed to sharing with the audiences the urgency they felt about the things they had to say. Yes? And that sharing, I don't think it's a terribly conscious thing. It is a need some people have, and then if it can be received, okay, fine; if it isn't received, well, then, there's frustration. But this is, I believe, what motivates us, what gets us there. And it's very obvious. The maturity in the person will indicate where he's at, at what particular place in his career.

SIEGEL: I think an audience really does perceive it. I don't think you need special codes and special training to get it, to pick it up. However, I think too many don't because they are entertainment-oriented. They are bombarded all the time about personalities, about the high jumps, and about the gossip—why did he switch companies? And is he going to do all right? And, gee, do you think he looks unhappy? And, wow, I wonder if they're sleeping together. And all that stuff.

As for the novice audience, which is what I think your question, Jerry, is about . . . they're really being fed that kind of junk, you know, and they think that's what it's about, because most of them come from the commercial theater. Dance as an art form just isn't part of the culture. Some people do get the kinaesthetic understanding, but they may deny it; they may submerge it; they may not reckon with it. They may decide it's about how high Baryshnikov jumps, when it may not be about that at all. I think it takes some elaborating. The more you see something the more you can see in it, if it's good, if it has content, but I think that's not something we can really expect dance audiences to have. They don't see any given thing long enough, or often enough, with the same dancers. I mean, even a critic very seldom can go back enough times to the same thing to really understand it deeply. That is why film is so useful to a critic. So maybe we have to find ways to revalue the art itself, to say more about what this thing is about, what's in it that you do perceive, that you're picking up, that you think isn't valuable, or that you don't think is the main thing you are to look at. Does that make sense?

MYERS: Very good sense. But we have to explain why some people get so intensely gratified by watching a dance concert. And so I think Maxine suggests that when you look at the experience people are having, there are features of that experience that maybe even the dancer as well as the audience don't quite understand. The dancers may be too busy having a high on stage. The critic has her eye on certain important features of the dance and perhaps is less interested in what you might call a psychological investigation of the experience the people in the seats are having. But Maxine is saying—if those people in the seats reflect upon their experience and begin to reflect on why they're so excited and why it's such an intense response they're having to the dance, then they'll find all sorts of things in the way of self-discovery. Do I understand that correctly, Maxine?

GREENE: Yes, and in addition I'm terribly eager to teach in such a way and to expose people to things in such a way that they're free to choose new opportunities for experiencing. I have the feeling people are manipulated on all sides by the things Marcia talked about, by television, by education as well, so the idea of somehow becoming aware of your own consciousness, of being able to think about your own thinking, seems to me to be a corrective against the sense of being worked on from outside.

AUDIENCE: What I want to know from Maxine Greene is if

dance can exist on a direct level, if an artist can create a dance on a direct level, facilitating an emotional experience in the spectator without necessitating this so-called educated eye? It seems if we choreograph simply for an educated audience, an audience of dancers, dance will remain for many people a mysterious art form; it will remain something on PBS rather than on CBS; it's going to stay in small halls. We've seen an incredible increase in dance audiences around the country, but I wonder if choreographers from New York really understand spectators in Dayton, Ohio.

GREENE: This may be my philosophic prejudice, but it seems to me the kind of emotional response that's evoked often depends on what you're able to perceive. In other words, you're responding to what you see. If this were not a culture so dominated by sensory bombardment of the kind that blinds people and keeps them from hearing, I wouldn't think it was so important to help people notice what there is to notice. If there were not so much stereotyping, and if fantasy life were not being crippled to the extent it is being crippled in children, I wouldn't see so much importance in helping people notice. When I say education I don't mean reading Aristotle. I really mean just trying to point, trying to disclose, not giving them the whole theoretical apparatus to do it, just trying to develop some sort of language, a few notes that might help people see better. If someone comes up and says—I loved it, I cared about it, I was excited by it—what's wrong with that? Do I have to know something, too? I can't say there's anything wrong with it. I can only be pleased, but at the same time I can also suggest there are always new possibilities. I think teaching is in part about always going a little beyond.

SIEGEL: Do you want me to answer you, too? I feel language is important. The intellectual process is essential. I have been teaching a course, mostly in observation for dancers, and I make them write, not because I think they're going to be writers or they want to be writers, but because writing it down gets you into the questions. Why did I love it? Why did I hate it? If you only maintain that level of shock reaction or gross like or dislike or whatever it is most people come out of a dance concert with, then you get so you can't discriminate. One of the great things about art is how varied it is, how much nuance it has, how much detail it has, how many things it can appeal to and how much depth it has in it. If everything is "I loved it" or "I hated it," you lose all of that, and I think ultimately you deny the quality of the artist. You deny what the artist really is about if you say "I loved Doris Humphrey" and "I loved Pilobolus" and "I loved Twyla Tharp" and "I loved Jerome Robbins." But none of these are anything like each other.

As a verbal person to begin with, not as a dancer, I went through a whole stage of saying—"words, no; movement, good." Forget about the words, just feel moved. And I do believe we can only connect with those things by moving and by understanding ourselves as moving beings. And giving ourselves permission, especially men in our culture, to move expressively and to understand what that is, not as dancers, just as walking-around people. That's another part of our educational process that is being ignored. But we went too far in putting down the words. We are intelligent beings and we're not just visceral things, things that feel. We do think and we should use that medium to connect with our own feelings and to connect ourselves to the arts we see.

DEBORAH JOWITT: I agree with Marcia and Maxine Greene in their plea for a kind of intensified seeing, but I worry that a lot of people think of that as a specialized form of seeing, and I was a little bothered, perhaps I didn't understand you correctly. When you began talking about distancing, you had just been talking about the mad scene in *Giselle*, and you used the word ordinary as if the kind of seeing you were talking about involved getting away from the ordinary and being transported. I don't know if I took your meaning right, but when I think of intensifying feeling, I don't think of it as different. I think if I couldn't recognize in *Giselle* its similarities or deformations from ordinary human movement, then I wouldn't be able to appreciate it at all, and I worry a lot that audiences think looking at dance involves some kind of special knowledge, a special way of looking and of perceiving.

GREENE: When I talk about distancing, I'm using it in the traditional sense. I mean uncoupling from one's practical concerns or from one's psychology book back home. I mean establishing oneself in a different psychic relation to what's happening on the stage. That's really all I mean. I do think there has to be a kind of awareness involved for people to do that, to move into an imaginary round, so they don't rush on the stage to save Desdemona. It's really a mystery to me, how it is we "discover" in this imaginary round that is different from the ordinary, how it results in such an illumination of the ordinary. That's the mystery to me. What is there about engagement in the uncommon that clarifies our common life? But the idea of distancing obviously is not mine. That's all I meant.

AUDIENCE: I'm someone who isn't exposed to all the gossip columns or the criticism and I don't read the New York papers, and I have two or three questions. The first is to Marcia Siegel in her talking about dance as a product. I'm not familiar with what that could be as opposed to dance as an art form. Secondly, there's been a lot of confusion about what Miss Greene meant in saying you shouldn't look at dance analytically but qualitatively instead. Yet you all seem to want to put some sort of conceptual framework between the audience and the dancer, and that leads to my third question. Where is their conceptual framework coming from? What are we as audience supposed to read? Does it stem from 400 years ago, and must we look at ballet one way but modern dance another way?

HOVING: You didn't hear me say that.

After looking at dance, what does it mean to me? Fifty years ago or more, when I wasn't yet dancing, I saw a dance, and I got involved with dance, was confronted with dance as a piano player in Holland. I remember a performance where I saw a simple gesture, arms over the head, and it freaked me out then. Thursday night in *Untitled* (Pilobolus) I saw Alison Chase do the same gesture and it freaked me out again. After more than fifty years of looking at dance, I still had a strong reaction. I cannot explain why it hits some people and why it does not hit other people. It's a mystery to me. I often read reviews and I don't agree with them but I don't necessarily get a complex that—"Oh, God, I have to learn . . . I know too little. . . ." I don't think people should develop complexes like that.

SIEGEL: I agree with you, Lucas, and I think that's what Deborah is talking about. There isn't a separate language for dance. If you see somebody opening their arms, you don't have to say, what does that mean? What is that gesture saying? What is that step and what is the step after that? What does *that* mean? Because it doesn't have that kind of relationship. What it does have is a kinaesthetic relationship that, if we're open to our own experience of movement and to our own sensations, we share with the dancer. Now, how far you detail it and how much you break it down, and how much you understand the context and the history and the resonance and all the rest of it, have to do with your education or what your background is. But the basic connection with dance has no special preconceptions about it.

I had never seen any dance until 1962 and I saw a lot of modern dance that summer, including Lucas, and I thought it was fantastic. I didn't have any trouble understanding it at the level I was at then, and I didn't understand why other people seemed to think it was strange and remote and difficult, because it wasn't difficult to me, and I think it was simply that it spoke to my basic responses. Later they became much more complicated, I now find I can't tolerate a lot of stuff I could tolerate then, but that doesn't have anything to do with where it starts from.

GREENE: Just one thing you've been talking about—the conceptual framework and its relation to perception. It's a common-sense, taken-for-granted way of looking at that building to see it as a dorm, a building that is used at Duke University to house students. Another way of looking at it is to see the qualities of the redness and the brick and the solidity and the difference between the shingles and the brick and so on, a sensitivity to the qualitative dimension of the world. I believe this can be provoked in some people. But I think some people, like Lucas, are born with it. There are people who naturally have that sort of tuning in to gesture, to the qualitative. But many other people have been so deafened and blinded that they see things for their use-value only, or they see *Giselle* as a psychological case. And I think we must say enough and provide enough concepts so people are freer to respond to color, to movement and to the imaginary. But it's not a heavy conceptual structure and to me its relevance is a function of its contribution to vision. It's not getting a doctorate in conception about dance. It's a different kind of relevance.

AUDIENCE: I would like to direct one question relative to the television workshop and to the critics' conference. How do you think television has affected and will continue to affect the aesthetic literacy you spoke of at the beginning of the conference?

GREENE: I think it can and it should, but again, I think we have to take responsibility in several ways. For one thing, I think it's good, obviously, that dance is on television—certainly better than if it were not. I think we all have to think about how the choices are made and by whom and who's involved, and I think the public has to understand much more about what is becoming immortal, and what is being left in the dark. I also think that because we have done so little about television literacy, we have to do something about that so people can respond with some kind of informed awareness to dance on television. But again, I think it's a whole new world we have to understand and don't understand yet. And I just want to say, a dance on television is not a dance in the theater. It adds another set of problems.

SIEGEL: I have often thought dance on TV is treated as if it were information, and it's televised for its information qualities and not for its art qualities. It's clear to me the same art qualities cannot come across on television that come across on the stage, but television does have its own aesthetic possibilities, as Merce Cunningham and Twyla Tharp have shown in their television work. I think it can be another experience entirely which we haven't even begun to explore the possibilities of.

Do You See What the Critic Sees?

Presented by
Gerald E. Myers

JAMES THURBER, cartoonist and illustrator, some years ago recounted an amusing anecdote of his undergraduate years at Ohio State University. He wrote of his difficulties in passing a laboratory course, due to his inability to see what was on the slide under the microscope. But one day he jubilantly summoned the laboratory instructor, flourishing his drawing of what he had finally discerned through the microscope, exclaiming "Look, at last I've got it!" The instructor spent a considerable time, obviously puzzled, in comparing Thurber's drawing with what was on the slide, and then declared, "Thurber, you know what you've done, you've drawn an image of your own eye."[1]

The Thurber anecdote illustrates the point that what is there to be seen is not always so easily perceived. It illustrates the thesis that seeing is partly determined by expectation, by theory, hypothesis or

33

guiding idea. Seeing is inevitably affected by what one brings to the act of seeing; it never occurs without the influence of prior knowledge or antecedent preconceptions. As many of us can appreciate from similar experiences, Thurber's eyes foundered because he had no prior idea of what he was supposed to see under the microscope.

Philosophers are chronically interested in the topic of seeing. Bertrand Russell developed a theory of perception the consequence of which is that what we all see are not things "out there" but are rather happenings in our own brains. He also argued that when you see the sun, since it took about ten minutes for the light to travel from the sun to your eyes, what you see really occurred ten minutes ago. Since all seeing depends upon light, and upon light taking *some* time to travel from even the nearest object to your eyes, what you see is always in the past, Russell concluded, and never in the actual present. The responses of numerous philosophers, of course, is that any theory of vision that has such odd consequences must be false.

Reading the distinguished dance critic, Arlene Croce, I am reminded of theories such as Russell's. In explicating the title of her book, *Afterimages*, she writes:

> Afterimage is defined as "the impression retained by the retina of the eye, or by any other organ of sense, of a vivid sensation, after the external cause has been removed." An afterimage is what we are left with when the performance is over. Dancing leaves nothing else behind—no record, no text—and so the afterimage becomes the subject of dance criticism. A dance critic tries to train the memory . . . to make the afterimage that appears in his writing match the performance. But often it doesn't match literally. . . .[2]

I understand Ms. Croce to acknowledge that, because dance is a peculiar art form, the dance critic is in a somewhat peculiar position. She would have us appreciate the ephemeral nature of a dance performance; no record or text is left. The drama critic can compare a production of Ibsen with the script, or the music critic can discuss an interpretation of Satie after studying the score. But the dance, as Merce Cunningham has reportedly said, is like water running through one's fingers, and so the dance critic, after the performance, returns home empty-handed, with only afterimages to consult in preparing a review.[3] It is because a dance performance is such a transient thing that the "afterimage becomes the subject of dance criticism." When the critic's memory is accurate, whether through training or happy coincidence, her review reports not only present memory images but the past performance as well.

Ms. Croce, unlike Russell, does not claim that what we see is in our heads, but she does resemble him in suggesting that what all spectators of dance, most notably critics, *criticize* is in our heads, namely, afterimages. The very nature of dance requires that the *subject* of dance criticism be memory images. But this, I think, is the philosophical leak in an otherwise intact account. What Croce intended as a sensitive testimonial to the nature of a dance performance, and as a frank confession of the critic's predicament, emerges as an unnecessarily paradoxical thesis. For, initially, note that, merely because you must use your memory in reporting how you dined, you are normally reporting something remembered, not something that occurs in the remembering. (You can resurrect the dinner no more than you can the ballet, but nothing in the nature of dinners requires that the subject of "dinner-criticism" be sapid afterimages.) We depend upon memory at every moment of our lives, but it would be shockingly paradoxical to suggest that the *subject* of our memory-dependent reports are the memories themselves. Moreover, if "images" are not to overpower us with their attractiveness, we should note that, normally, we do not check a memory-claim against a present memory image, but rather vice versa. Is my present image of a remembered lady a good one? When I try to answer this, I seem to rely on a memory that may not consist of images at all. I just recall, that is all, and I may be wholly unable to espy any present images. Hence, if the dance critic works with vivid memory images, she will need to "check" them to determine if they match the witnessed performance; if so, why not abandon the idea that, due to dance's special nature, afterimages rather than the actual performances are the subject matter of dance criticism?

Lucas Hoving, I suspect, is depressed when told that not he but a critic's *afterimage* of him is what is reviewed. Lucas, remembering certain reviews, may not be so surprised to hear this, yet it merely deepens his depression. Thus, if only to relieve a dancer's melancholy, we ought, if we can, to repair that philosophical leak in Ms. Croce's account. Let us agree that the performance, not the memory of it, is the subject of dance criticism. Dance critics are not in some peculiar predicament, trapped in current images that may or may not relate to an unbridgeable past. As we all constantly do, they, too, in their functions, must rely on memory, not, however, for making

35

inbred reports on remembering experiences themselves but rather on what is being remembered. Accurate memory is precisely the bridge between past and present, so we must resist interpreting it as being nothing more than present, bridgeless images. Reinstating the performance as the proper subject matter for dance criticism can buoy the dancer depressed by the "afterimage" alternative; it can also enthuse aesthetics throughout with a respect for the art work itself. What is troublesome about aesthetic or critical notions that give center stage to images, illusions and the like, is that the primary thing, the art work itself, gets removed to some dreamy image world—or so it seems.[4] Because Ms. Croce's equating the subject of dance criticism with afterimages can lend support to that troublesome, subjectivistic tradition in aesthetics, it seemed worthwhile to register a demurrer here. Turning to the titular question of this discussion, let us note in particular that, if the critic's evaluation focuses upon afterimages, the likelihood increases that what we see at a dance performance differs from what the critic writes about in her review. There is sufficient difficulty already in insuring that we see the same thing, but, if what we see must match her special memory images, the difficulty is obviously aggravated.

II.

We rightly wonder whether we see what the critics see, because they are experts, and they too often do see what we overlook. We constantly learn from dance critics how to see performances in enriched ways. For example, take Deborah Jowitt's comments on last spring's production of Balanchine's ballet *Apollo*. She explains how Balanchine has repeatedly pruned earlier versions of the ballet and how Baryshnikov's performance represents a new kind of Apollo. At one point, Ms. Jowitt writes, when the three lovely Muses "parade across the back of the stage, and he whacks each of them like the fillies they are, the action startles us . . . what Baryshnikov presents us with is not so much the young reckless Apollo becoming mature . . . but Dionysus becoming Apollo."[5] Knowing the facts and interpretations provided by Jowitt enable us to see the ballet more fully, more accurately, more confidently. Or, in the early Seventies, some of us were helped in watching Meredith Monk's dances by critics such as Don McDonagh. He observed that Monk was creating an "ongoing process theater"; each new work of hers borrowed or included material from the preceding one. "She attempts to link recurring artistic materials with the diverse places in which she finds herself. Her work becomes, in effect, an artistic autobiography."[6] Supplied with this insight, one looked at Monk's productions with new eyes, noticing things previously ignored and reassessing moments in those productions which had before been merely baffling or frustrating.

We can wonder, however, whether we see what the critics see, because, notoriously, the critics may themselves not see alike. Marcia Siegel writes: "Seeing is a very selective, individual and concrete process, and it means to me more than mere opinion. Nancy Goldner, Arlene Croce and Deborah Jowitt can all see different things than I did in a dance we all liked."[7] And Arlene Croce has scolded fellow critics for being "eyeless," especially when observing stars such as Erik Bruhn. She once complained that critics, much like the astigmatic public, were bravoing Bruhn when, in fact, he was quite obviously indulging in some weird goofiness on stage.[8] So we can become anxious that our seeing may be blinded, not only by the bright lights of our own idiosyncracies, but by the aura of the stars we're watching. Besides, of course, there is a problem, in watching dance, of keeping your eye on all that is happening. A large company and production can create a very busy stage, and, when the action is brisk, you are taxed to see it all—and equally; for it is easy to tarry your gaze on one dancer, or on one part of the stage, and during that period you neglect the rest. Distributing one's attention evenly over an extravagant ballet is a singular achievement. Our untrained looking can understandably fall short of the professional critic's viewing, and even for her the "busyness" of dance can interrupt the effort to attend equally. To see equally and to see selectively are virtually contradictory.

We can also wonder whether we see "critically," because so often what critics and devotees of the dance see are "qualities" of movement. *Qualities of movement*—this concept is my central topic this evening. Certainly, there is much more to the art of dance, there is the overarching choreography, the use of music, costumes, props, lighting, and there are the relations between performers, the special adaptations of space and time, and so on. But I shall confine my reflections to movement qualities, because they are, I believe, if anything is, the "bottom-liners" in an exposition of what is special about the art of dancing. What I have in mind as "qualities" of movement can be gotten at by quoting contrasting passages from our critic, Marcia Siegel. She has written about a Laura Dean performance as follows:

> Facing the audience in a nicely-spaced formation, the dancers do a whole series of combinations in place that incorporates ballet steps—entrechats, ronds de jambe—in canon and with different rhythmic accents. There's a glimpse of a tap dancer's time step. Suddenly they look as if they're doing some kind of balletic Hungarian folk dance. At another moment they're gliding around on bent knees like Balinese court dancers. The rond de jambe becomes a Charleston kick.[9]

This is first-rate reporting, a wonderful verbal picture of the performance. But it does not (save possibly for "gliding") mention what I am calling "qualities" of movement. Fine description that successfully pictures what occurred on stage may yet omit an even more "finely-tuned" description of movement qualities. In a different place Ms. Siegel makes an extremely interesting observation about the relation between José Limón and Lucas Hoving:

> The drama of equal adversaries was the formula for Limón's long and successful partnership with Lucas Hoving. . . . Theirs was a performing relationship one seldom finds in dance; so much more often we remember man-woman duos, or even trios. . . . But Limón never became as closely associated with a woman partner as he did with Hoving . . . if José Limón wasn't dancing solo, he seems to have needed the strength and size of another man to match his own.[10]

This moves closer to a mention of movement qualities—"strength" and "size" are suggestive—but we must turn to Siegel's most recent book, *The Shapes of Change,* for a more explicit mention of what interests us here. "Neither man was really a sensual dancer, but where Hoving was balletically vertical and rather brittle in his movement, Limón was tight and strong."[11] She appeals to movement qualities also in characterizing with high praise the dancing of Gelsey Kirkland, referring to this dancer's "terrific lightness, fluidity and delicacy, but also her restraint."[12] Each of these words alludes to what I understand as a "movement quality." Besides the dancer's movements, then, there are the qualities of these movements, and what we notice, when studying the talk of dancers and dance critics, is how much emphasis is placed upon *qualities* when appreciation and evaluation are being expressed. Two dancers may execute pretty much the same movement, but one is praised over the other, for the reason, say, that hers was "fluid" whereas the other's was "fudged." In all the arts the basic item of appreciation is "aesthetic quality"—the quality of the brush stroke, the quality of the sound, the quality of the oral delivery, and so on. In dance, it is the quality of movement.

III.

Philosophical questions are provoked by our concept of movement qualities. There is, first, the troublesome vagueness of words such as "light," "fluid," "tight," "brittle," "restrained," etc., as applied to human movement. The philosopher wants to know what is involved in coming to understand what one means by describing movement in such terms. Besides vagueness, outright disagreement can occur; what critic A calls "floaty," critic B calls "driftless." We then confront the question, if such qualities attach to the dancer's movements, why are we, as amateur viewers, quite apt to overlook them, and why can the critics, the expert viewers, dispute them? Why is it that, until Marcia Siegel talks to me about Kirkland's dancing, I fail to see the quality of "restraint"—but then, suddenly, I do see it? We can all see that a movement is slow, everyone (with normal vision) can see that a book is brown, a surface shiny, a substance thick. Yet we may debate vigorously whether a dancer's dancing is "fluid" or not. Lincoln Kirstein once wrote of David Lichine's performance in Fokine's *Le Spectre de la Rose:* ". . . Lichine's interpretation of the Rose exemplifies only too nakedly what superficial ballet technique accomplishes. All that was once movement, smooth and simple as honey, is now broken, gauche, saccharine and pretentious."[13] Though the adjectives here demand some interpreting perhaps, they evidently refer to movement qualities. Now, how could Lichine have defended himself? How could the debate between him and Kirstein be resolved? Just by more seeing, and by whom?

A philosophical dilemma threatens: either we conclude that qualities of movement are "objective" features of the dancer's movements, in which case they must seem to be extraordinarily elusive things, available only to godlike eyes, else how could our most astute critics miss or dispute them? And it does seem odd that movements on stage, in full view, should own such terribly elusive aspects. Or—to avoid this conclusion—we might jump to the other, that it is merely a matter of taste; movement qualities, like beauty, are only in the beholder's eye. So the qualities are catalogued among afterimages, illusions, visions and other subjective things. But suppose Lucas Hoving and all of us concur that Ms. Siegel is correct, his movement in a certain dance was "brittle"; Lucas is delighted that we find in his dancing a quality he rehearsed for hours to achieve. It does seem strange, however, to tell him the quality is merely an image or illusion in the heads of us spectators. If we take this line, we only succeed in depressing Lucas again.

What I would emphasize is how one's thinking can so easily and imperceptibly swing to and fro on the issue. At one moment you are confident that "qualities" are truly objective, inherently attached features of the individual's dancing. The "liquidity" of the ballerina's *glissades* sometimes appears obvious to your gaze; moreover, the audience generally testifies to it; everyone congratulates everyone on the good fortune of witnessing it, so it seems ridiculous for you not to suppose that the "liquidity" literally belongs to the dancer's movements as her feet literally belong to her body. Indeed, according to the testimony of professional dancers, it is usually some special quality of the movement, not just the movement itself, that attracts their attention in watching a performance. If so, then the objectivity or "out-thereness" of the quality seems even further assured. You never assert that the softness of the cloth you purchase is purely subjective, a quality of your response to the cloth rather than of the fabric itself. Why, then, contend that the "lyric" quality of an individual's dancing belongs to your response rather than to the dancing itself? Once we understand how our everyday thinking is undecided on the issue, how it vacillates uneasily between objectivistic and subjectivistic interpretations of aesthetic qualities, we can all the more appreciate how a tendency by critics and aestheticians to resort to "images," "illusions" and the like, can almost surreptitiously direct our minds towards the subjectivistic conception of the art work and its unique aesthetic qualities. On the other hand, a militaristically confident declaration by a self-assured critic that a certain dancer moves "woodenly" can set us to thinking the quality is really there, as objectively "there" in the movement as your nose is "there" on your face. Thus, depending on the context, your mood, the degree of audience agreement, the type of critic with whom you converse at intermission, because you float so eratically between objectivism and subjectivism, you will on a specific occasion opt for one polar interpretation of qualities but on another occasion you will argue for just its opposite.

Do not underestimate how seductive subjectivism is. For one thing, it is philosophically *easier*. You say, "His dancing is 'ragged.' " Friends and critics boo your judgment, and you find yourself retreating to, "Well, it *struck* me as 'ragged' " (or it "seemed . . .," "felt . . .," "made me think of . . .," "gave me the impression of being . . .," "reminded me of . . .," "suggested to me . . .," and the like). These retreated-to judgments abandon the original, objectivistic claim that the dancing *is* ragged, for you are now content to maintain merely that the "raggedness" belongs somehow to your response rather than to the dancing. These retreated-to judgments are much easier to defend; you are relieved of trying to prove the dancing *is* ragged, and, after all, who wants to quarrel with your merely confessional remark that the dancing caused you to respond or feel in such a way that you allude to it with the word "ragged"? Everyone is prepared to admit your right to your own responses, even if the admission is hedged with murmurs that, given greater sophistication and experience, your responses might become more appropriate. The fact remains that, when challenged, it is argumentatively easier, often pleasanter, to retreat to a judgment that transfers the aesthetic quality from the artistic object to one's responses to that object.

There is also what I take to be the sociological fact, namely, that artists themselves, while perhaps assuming the aesthetic qualities they find in their own works are really objectively *there*, are prepared to argue that the qualities allegedly discerned by the critics are only subjective features of the critics' responses. This is partly due to their acclimation to being at odds with critical assessments of their works and to their resignation to the omnipresent fact of debates between critics continuing unresolved. Hence, confronted by a critic's evaluation, the artist shrugs it off with, "Each critic sees it his or her own way." It is remarkable how many artists simply assume that different critics will see their works differently, and that, therefore, the qualities which the critics claim to see in those works are instead aspects of the critics' responses. The verdict of the artistic community is a huge vote, it seems, for subjectivism, insofar as it applies to criticism anyway. This is a fact to be remembered if one seeks to make a case for objectivism.

Some critics will vote with the artists here. They say criticism has certain facts to report—time, place, date, the identities of performers, historical background notes, certain points of comparison, and so on; but beyond such factual reporting, there is a job of evaluation or criticism to be done, and this includes discussion of "qualities." Evaluation or criticism, these critics concede, is indeed largely subjective, but that is not a cause for complaint. For look at the matter in this light: some dancers are more interesting personalities than others on stage; they project more vividly and fascinate our gaze. Equally, some critics are more intriguing personalities than others in print, and although what they "see" for criticism is mainly from their own point of view, nevertheless, just because they invigorate our reading and perhaps our viewing, they are laudable for the interest excited by and through their subjective biases. Accordingly, if a critic assesses a dancer as displaying a "warm," "airy," "fluid," but slightly "affected" movement style, in the specific context that judgment may sway us, not because we believe the mentioned qualities are genuinely objective features of the dancing, but because we find the critic as interesting as the dancing. If he or she has responses that include such qualities, then maybe we will or ought to also. The critic who truly values his or her own responses, who treats them as good indices of taste and aesthetic judgment, is quite untroubled by a subjectivistic interpretation of qualities. Looking at the matter in this light, we can envision subjectivism as actually revising and upgrading our notion of the critic. Between them, artist and critic, they can make a formidable front for subjectivism.

But, before surrendering to it, we should ask some basic questions. What *is* subjectivism; what does it actually claim? For instance, if it holds that my judgment, say, that a movement is "liquid" or "wooden" is really a report that "liquid" and "wooden" are qualities of my response, then it seems quite false. These words obviously do not refer to how I feel in watching the movement; it is obviously the movement that strikes me as liquid or wooden, not my own feelings. Moreover, I have no idea what a "liquid" feeling could be. So there can be no temptation here to invoke an esoteric perceptual theory which treats aesthetic qualities as things that we mysteriously "project" from within ourselves onto the "out-there" world. The words "liquid" and "wooden" do not even seem to refer to anything in my response, and, if the subjectivist insists that nevertheless they do refer to such, either we do not understand him or his reasoning is buried in mystery. We must reject that version of subjectivism which holds that the words used for referring to aesthetic qualities "really" refer to qualities of our responses.

A more plausible brand of subjectivism is this: when you call a movement "hectic," you are really reporting what the movement causes you to think of or to associate with it; you do not literally find something hectic in the movement, but there is something about the movement that brings the idea of "hectic" to mind. The idea, of course, is subjective, and it, on this version of subjectivism, is what is alluded to by "hectic." But, again, our rebuttal points out that you are not, even slightly, referring to an idea in calling the movement "hectic." Certainly the idea of hectic is prompted in you by seeing the movement, but it is yet the movement, not that idea, which plays subject to the predicate "hectic." Thus, the theory must at least be amended somewhat as follows: something S in the dancer's movements causes you to think of "hectic," and it is S which, because of your associating it with being hectic, is metaphorically described by you as "hectic." S is not literally but only metaphorically hectic, given your particular subjective associations. This is plausible, even attractive, insofar as it seems to explain, first, how critical disagreement is due to differences in subjective associations, and, secondly, how words for aesthetic qualities can only be understood as special metaphors.

This version of subjectivism might succeed, if the critic could normally identify straightforwardly S, that is, if the critic could identify directly what it is "in" or "about" the movement that prompts him or her to apply "wooden" to the movement. If you associate a certain wine with a particular friend, then you normally have no problem in identifying both terms of this associative relation. When that wine is put before you and that friend comes to mind, you can, if needed, directly indicate what it is that makes you think of him. But the critic, I believe, is not typically presented with such straightforward associative relations. The critic's attitude is inadequately reported by "See that movement—I associate it and its kind with 'wooden.' " For one thing, saying that commits the critic to an unbelievable generalization, namely, that no matter what the context is, that type of movement is associated with woodenness. You will find, I think, that the critic (amateur and professional) typically says something more like this: "There is something *in* or *about* the movement that makes me apply 'wooden' to it." He or she will probably reject your invitation to call it a case of association, not wanting to say, "That feature S of the movement is something I associate with woodenness." There are two good reasons for his or

43

her not wanting to say this. One is that the critic does not really discern any associative relation resembling that between the wine and a friend. The other is, when the critic tries to identify S, she will probably concede—insist—she is unable to point to some specific feature S of the movement and say, "It is *that*, just that and nothing else, which brings 'wooden' to mind." Trying to identify a specific quality S of the movement in virtue of which the latter is called "wooden" is as elusive a task as was the original one of seeking to locate in the movement the wooden quality itself. For these reasons, I conclude the customary behavior of the critic sufficiently refutes, despite its initial plausibility, this version of subjectivism.

What favors objectivism? First, we avoid depressing the dancer through arguing that the qualities of movement which he rehearses diligently to achieve are merely features of the spectator's responses, by urging, to the contrary, that such qualities are as objective as the movement itself. Secondly, some movement qualities do in fact impress all of us with their objectivity: light, heavy, rapid, slow, continuous, jerky, expansive, contracted and so on. True, we sometimes quarrel about the presence of these, but generally we accept their objectivity. Given the "out-there" reality of some qualities, granting similar status to others such as "fluid," "wooden," etc., meets less resistance. Thirdly, where we flatly differ with the critic or do not grasp what she means by "hard-edged" or "brittle," we are more likely to resolve our differences and understand the critic's meaning by focusing upon the dancer's movement rather than upon the subjective details of our and the critic's responses. By studying the movement and noticing what the critic tends to call "fluid" or "steely," we have a better chance of locating what it is in or about the movement that she notices. This consorts, of course, with the fact that the critic, after all, sets out to report the movement as the main event, her particular responses being something of a side show.

But, having said this, can we explain the apparent variability and elusiveness of aesthetic qualities in a manner consistent with objectivism? If we can, nothing remains to prevent our accepting it. I shall attempt the outline of an explanation, although the details and the "mechanics" are certainly beyond my competence, perhaps beyond everyone's. The explanation proceeds on the premise that thinking and seeing are somehow intertwined, or, as William Blake said, to see only with the eye is to believe a lie.[14] More than the physical eye is involved in seeing the "wooden" quality of the dancer's movement, as more than the physical eye was required for Thurber to see the microorganism on the slide. We must think in a certain way, be in a certain frame of mind, before the "lyric" quality can be perceived. This in no way implies that the quality is merely subjective, a thing in the spectator's mind; it is a genuinely objective feature of the dancer's performance, but it is not an isolated item you can see if you just cock your head, narrow your eyes, etc. To see a movement now as "brittle" but then as "hard-edged" is obviously to undergo a radical visual alteration; it involves a significant redescription and re-thinking of the movement and is not simply spotting one isolated quality in place of another; that is, it is not like hearing a loud bang, then a soft whine. The change is more subtle than this, the quality occurring as an inseparable part of a larger context and not capable of being isolated from that context for separate identification. When you see the lyric quality of the dancing, you cannot, even in imagination, detach the lyric quality from the dancing for independent consideration, because it is too much a perceptual "part" of the dancing itself. It is "in" the movement rather like a pain can be "in" one's knee; you don't find the lyric quality by dissecting the movement any more than you can point to something that is the pain by surgically opening up the knee.

I noted earlier my reasons for preferring objectivism, but recall what is at stake. Subjectivism tends to shift the focus from performance to criticism, from dancer to critic. It creates a schism between art and criticism, one that can depress the artist while inclining the critic to think of her own contribution as self-contained, a work of art in itself. Insofar as subjectivism views aesthetic qualities as belonging to the subjective responses of the spectator, it divides what the critic sees, not merely from what we see, but also from what the dancer does. If our philosphy of art, however, places aesthetic qualities at center stage and intends them to be publicly and commonly perceptible, to critic and amateur viewer alike, and if it intends the art work itself (which, note, is defined largely via its specific aesthetic qualities) to be the focus of critical viewing, then we have the incentive to make the strongest case possible for objectivism.

I asserted above that a quality is not subjective merely because its presence is detected only if one thinks in a certain way or is in a certain frame of mind. This needs elaborating, since there is a philosophical prejudice that, if something is perceptually objective, it will look the same, no matter what frame of mind one is in. Unless one is mentally deranged, there is no mistaking the perceptual fact of a person on stage dancing, so that much of the scene is clearly objective. But the color of the costume, is that objective? Some philosophers have replied negatively, on the grounds that color is too variable, changing when the lighting changes, when the atmosphere changes, and so on. If the alleged objectivity of color is menaced, how much more in jeopardy are such movement qualities as "wooden" and "fluid." I agree, the blue of the costume is normally more obvious to more people than is the "wooden" quality of the movement, so if the blue is argued to be subjective, so must "wooden" also. But the blue, I submit, is *not* subjective; unlike headaches, thoughts, dreams, moods, feelings and bodily sensations, colors usually characterize external things and thus do not tempt us to re-locate them within our responses. Colors are normally unlike hallucinations, for example, which are evidently subjective, although occasionally, if a perception of color occurs in the apparent absence of anything external displaying that color, we do classify it as illusory or hallucinatory. But, for sound reasons, we are never drawn to the idea that all colors are subjective. So much for the argument that, since colors are subjective, aesthetic qualities must certainly be the same.

Nevertheless, many if not most aesthetic qualities are admittedly more variable and elusive than the usual color qualities of ordinary things. The "skimming" quality of a dancer's movement is more akin to the "cool" quality of blue or to the "warm" quality of red than to the colors themselves. We agree that the costume is blue but maybe disagree that the blue is "cool." But, again, the variability of "cool" does not establish its subjectivity. What is shown is that our perception of "cool" and aesthetic qualities is more dependent upon our frame of mind, upon whether our perceiving emphasizes this or that feature of the thing we see, and upon, generally, our preconceptions. To illustrate, consider a particular person's smile, which you first perceive as "sympathetic," but then, suddenly, it strikes you as "sinister." This change in your perception can occur although the other's smile is physically unchanged. The change certainly seems to be objective; it definitely seems to be "out there," a change in the appearance of the physical smile, and it is not experienced as a change in your responses, in the way, for instance the change from sadness to joy is experienced as an alteration in oneself. Moreover, "sympathetic" and "sinister" refer to something in or about the person's smile, not to anything identifiable as your response to that smile. If I am uncertain what you mean by applying such words to the smile, wondering how you are using them metaphorically, my best chance of determining your meaning is to study, with your help, the actual appearance of that smile. If you are not quite certain yourself just what it is in the smile that prompts you to change your description of it from "sympathetic" to "sinister," you also need to concentrate on the smile; you may discover, for instance, that your earlier perceiving of it accented one aspect of it, whereas your later perceiving focused or emphasized another aspect, the difference in focus resulting in the change from "sympathetic" to "sinister." This points to the conclusion that what these words name are objective qualities but ones that are sensitively dependent upon slight changes in the perceptual circumstances. Things and scenes will display this or that aesthetic quality, but only if a rather fragile combination of factors occurs, and included in that combination is our psychological "set" or frame of mind.

At the same time, in explaining the change from "sympathetic" to "sinister," you may also inquire, not only into what there is in or about the smile itself that makes the change, but into what else may contribute to the alteration. And you may discover the cause was in part a change in your mind-set. This is not of course to find that the sinister quality is "in" your mind; it is rather to learn that your mental set is a condition for perceiving certain aesthetic qualities. Or, perhaps better, to vary the conditions of perception, including the perceiver's mind-set, is to vary the qualities which things "take on" or "drop off" for that perceiver. Expressing it this way emphasizes that the aesthetic qualities we notice, no matter how sensitively dependent they may be upon slight variations in perceptual conditions, being therefore highly variable as well as moderately elusive, are always perceived as qualifying things "out there"—as contrasted with headaches, moods, feelings and thoughts, which are not experienced as being "out there." The qualities are as genuinely among the ways in which things appear as are size, shape, color and so on. The compelling reason for maintaining the objectivity of aesthetic qualities is their sheer appearance of such; they obviously seem to be qualities *of* things, *of* movements and *of* scenes, and in the absence of any good theory that would show all of this to be merely illusory, we are justified in accepting the appearances. The world, that is, is as aesthetic as it is anything else, and as it is so it appears.

What fascinates the dancer and the dance critic, I believe, are movement qualities; these are *the* essential perceptual elements in the appreciation of dancing. That is why determining their objectivity or subjectivity is so important. There is another consideration worth noting in weighing the issue. It is true the dancer's performance is typically in the service of a larger choreography, and this larger thing can be called *the* art work. Yet a distinctive feature of the dance is that the dancer is always seeking to make his or her body and its movements an ongoing art work. It is off target to say, as often occurs, that the dancer uses his body as an instrument. The violinist uses his instrument to make music, which is separate from the violin; but the dancer uses his own body to make that body itself into the art work. The development of movement qualities "on" one's own body is as essential to being an art work as it is to servicing the choreography. The dancer is distinctive in being the very art work he or she creates.

Movement qualities are the result of personality, of height and weight, of involuntary mannerisms, of rehearsed efforts, of musical response, of the whole body, or of only isolated parts, and on and on. So much goes into the making of the qualities that define the particular art work that is the dancer himself. One must see and think a good deal to see subtle movement qualities. One must see as guided by a thinking that incorporates an understanding of dance technique, of choreographic tradition and innovation, of the relations of movement qualities to qualities found in the other arts, of "Effort-Shape" type of analyses, etc. So it is not strange that qualities of dance movements are "reasonably" elusive and can be easily overlooked by newcomers to the art; nor, given the subtlety involved, is it extraordinary that the experts, critics and dancers, can see differently. To see alike, to notice the same simultaneous and successive display of movement qualities "on" the dancer's body, in his movements, requires a similar mind-set. To see what is on a particular critic's microscopic slide involves sharing certain of her preconceptions as to what is being looked for and how one would recognize it. What is there to be seen may be reasonably elusive, but if the critics and we look at the same dance with similar preconceptions, we have a good chance of seeing that dance rather than, say, images of our own eyes.

You can understand, given my point of view, how happy I was to read a review of the recent Pilobolus performance by one of our own American Dance Festival stalwarts, Frank Jeffreys (with Jim Buie), which includes this: "The audience is taken in by some elemental quality found in the movement whether it is the emotional aspect, the quality, the texture or the sheer force found within the movement."[15] You may want more information about precisely what that "elemental quality" is that so impressed the reviewers. You may complain about the disconcerting vagueness of the words used to name the quality. Anna Kisselgoff has recently suggested a new vocabulary in dance criticism is needed; she asserts critics tend to repeat themselves in a tired language.[16] Perhaps a new vocabulary can be evolved that will incorporate the richness of background and concepts, the heterogeneous conceptual framework, required by us to see as the critic sees. In any event, whatever will assist the critic in conveying what she sees is to be encouraged. The critic, as the Greek word *kritikos* means, is one "able to discern or judge." The critic of quality is one who discerns quality.

IV.

Dance has become popular, prominent in American culture. Why? Popularity, however, can kill its own product, and Marcia Siegel, among others, is sometimes alarmed. Commenting on the rude, out-of-control audience responses to name performers, she writes: "A few years ago Alvin Ailey made a dance about the mutual turn-on and drag-down that stars and audiences exert over each other. It was suggested by the life of Janis Joplin and it starred Lynn Seymour [Maxine Sherman in the Ailey performance at the American Dance Festival, summer, 1979] and was called *Flowers*." Siegel continues: "It's all reminiscent somehow of the Kennedy era. Except I think what the mob wanted so desperately with the Kennedys was to believe they were common men. Now the crowd wants to believe in itself as star."[17] All part of the "Me Generation," is her idea, the cult of narcissism, the crowd consolidating itself into a grotesque, simultaneous ego trip.

Lincoln Kirstein sees the relation between ballet popularity and American culture somewhat differently. In a brilliant response to a "file-and-forget" survey, Kirstein writes that ballet frames morality in miniature, ballet performances presenting models of an ideal order. His tongue-in-cheek way of filling out the analogy is amusing

49

but ultimately serious. "Ballet is a secular rite; if it is well performed, the congregation applauds; detonations fuse in air; the God has appeared. There has been a transient manifestation of Order. . . . Order is what ballet is about. . . . In those of our theaters where ballet is housed with some continuity or stability, ballet performances present maps or models of an ideal civil state, the Republic, commonwealth: the City of God. They are communions of experts and enthusiasts, two-hour services celebrating mutuality of credence in something superior to the miserable I or Me. . . . the reason ballet has arrived in its impermanent permanency of popular acceptance is its transparent demonstration of the principles of service and order. As an increasingly accepted symbol of our society's spiritual preoccupations, it could be hardly less representative of an 'Age of Me.' "[18]

I noticed a small black girl in the audience at one of the recent Ailey performances in Page Auditorium. She was jumping in her seat to the music that blended Jelly Roll Morton, Sidney Bechet and Duke Ellington. Looking around, she seemed momentarily astonished to observe that the largely white audience, in the mezzanine rows behind her, must have resembled a cemetery-scene, stone-rigid in their seats. One asks, must we sit, frozen, with eyes riveted stageward, to see a dance? The stare of a dance audience that includes aficionados, former dancers, future dancers, students of leg movements, students of arm movements, fans of the human body, stargazers of the theatrical firmament—the stary seeing of that audience is absolutely ravenous. Nothing must interrupt the visual feast. Odd, how rigid must be the body that watches the dancer's body and its quicksilver succession of movement qualities. I conclude: to satiate the gluttonous seeing that devours every little quality of dancing, that nibbles at every morsel of movement quality left at the corners of the eyes, is to be as selfish or as narcissistic as the finest specimen of today's "Me Generation." But the sacrifice or denial of self, what is strikingly unrepresentative of our "Age-of-Me," is to be found, not in what we see at the ballet, nor in what it symbolizes, but rather in the cost to knees and lower back that we cheerfully pay for enduring in our auditorium seats what is a lengthy and rather military sit. Why do we endure it? To see those subtle, elusive qualities of the dancer's movements. The way things are, a body that moves is visually appreciated by a body that is still, very still.[19]

50

NOTES

1. I reconstruct this from memory, unfortunately unable to recall where the anecdote is to be found. Therefore, quoted remarks are obviously my own paraphrases.
2. *Afterimages*, Vintage, 1979, p. 2.
3. Interview reported in *The Durham Sun*, July 19, 1979.
4. This sort of criticism has been made of Susanne Langer, for instance, who exploits the idea of "illusion" in her *Feeling and Form*.
5. *The Village Voice*, May 21, 1979, p. 99.
6. *The New York Times*, July 20, 1970.
7. *Watching The Dance Go By*, Houghton Mifflin, 1977, p. xvi.
8. *Afterimages*, pp. 331-338.
9. *Watching The Dance Go By*, pp. 311-312.
10. Ibid., p. 161.
11. *The Shapes of Change*, Houghton Mifflin, 1979, p. 309.
12. *Watching The Dance Go By*, p. 20.
13. *New Theatre*, June 1936, p. 21.
14. I owe this reference to Blake to a mention of it by the dance critic, John Martin, in his column in *The New York Times*, March 31, 1957.
15. *Durham Morning Herald*, June 29, 1979.
16. *The Arts Journal*, Asheville, Vol. 4, No. 9, June, 1979, p. 7.
17. *Watching The Dance Go By*, p. 3.
18. "Ballet and the Public: Notes From A Diary," *The New York Review of Books*, 25:18-21, November 23, 1978.
19. The topic of aesthetic qualities is, of course, an important one in the literature of aesthetics. Three examples that come to mind are the following:
    Arnold Isenberg: "Critical Communication," originally published in *The Philosophical Review* (1949), and anthologized, for instance, in *Aesthetics and Language* (William Elton, ed.), 1954, pp. 131-146.
    Stephen C. Pepper: *Aesthetic Quality*, Charles Scribner and Sons, 1937.
    Leo Steinberg: "The Eye is a Part of the Mind," originally published in the *Partisan Review*, vol. 44, no. 2 (1953); reprinted in Susanne Langer (ed.), *Reflections on Art*, Oxford University Press, 1958, pp. 243-261.

DISCUSSION FOLLOWING
GERALD MYERS PRESENTATION

Panelists: Maxine Greene, Marcia Siegel,
Lucas Hoving, Gerald Myers

MAXINE GREENE: Why should anybody see as the critics see? Why shouldn't it be the job of critics to help us see through our own eyes? Another question I have is, can I really see brittle? I can see quality but do I see brittle? But I am curious to know what the critic finds in what she just heard and what the dancer finds in the problem of criticism.

GERALD MYERS: I said we don't see brittle as an isolated quality. But we do see the brittle quality in terms of a context. And it is there. The brittle quality is a part of the physical performance. It is part of the dancer's movement; it is not something in my head. It really is an objective part of the performance, but in order for me to see the brittle quality I must have a whole context at work. I suppose I am espousing something like a Gestalt theory of perception—that we see things as part of a context. But, at any rate, if you don't see the brittle quality but then a critic talks to you and, as a result, you do see the brittle quality and say, "How did I miss it? Now I understand what you are saying," I think that is due to the fact that you have rethought and redescribed what you are looking at, in the way in which Thurber was led to do, and then you see it. How you see is affected by how you're thinking about what you're looking at.

MARCIA SIEGEL: Jerry said the critic doesn't see without pre-conceptions or presuppositions, or that no one does. I don't agree. My goal in going to look at anything is to see it. Then I think about it. The optimum way for me to go and look at something is not to think about it at all. Of course you can't ever separate these two things, but optimally I would not like to exercise preconceptions. I would not like to exercise conceptions when I am looking at a dance. I would like to exercise my kinaesthetic response. I would like to exercise my visual sense, my emotional feeling response, my intellect in the sense of form and perceiving how things are growing, changing and happening. That's an entirely different system of work from the system that starts to operate when I sit down in front of my Olympia

52

Standard and attach my fingers to the keys. That is the thinking process and that's when that takes place. I do agree with the image of afterimages. We do work from afterimages.

You may be moved. You may be thrilled. You may be disgusted. You may be shocked. You may be tired. You may be a million things when you are watching the dance. But when you are writing or thinking about the dance all of that comes back and the dance comes back, hopefully. And then you think about it, and then you ask yourself what did that really look like, what did it make me think about, what qualities did it have, what made it different from some other thing, how can I use those words, how can I get this across? I think very few words have absolute meanings and I'm not looking for absolute meanings. I'm not trying to tell anybody any absolute truth, and I don't think—maybe I'm wrong—that the dancer wants to deliver us an absolute truth. In any case, I'm trying to illuminate my own mind, my own reaction. I think you are asking an awful lot if you expect the critic to put a dance into an intellectual framework that is perhaps more definite and more positive and more graspable than the experience itself. I don't think that is what critics really want to do. I do think they want to illuminate their own reactions and help you see how other people have reacted who may have seen more than you or may do it more often than you, and see if that is of any use to you.

LUCAS HOVING: First I want to ask Marcia something. Brittle? Was it *The Emperor Jones?*

SIEGEL: I was thinking a lot about that. Yes.

HOVING: Well, I've gone through my brittle period. Yeah, I didn't like that. I did not like it, but it was—yeah, the body. Okay, I have a terrible confession to make. I read reviews when I get a chance—hardly ever my own. I put them away for later, because I am very vulnerable when I am dancing something, and I don't necessarily want to read in black and white what a failure as a human being I am, because that's how we take it, you see. So I put them away, and when it's long enough ago I am not that interested anymore. But I have them.

I read other people's reviews. But I don't really feel like reading about dancing after a whole day of dancing. Enough is enough. But I want to say this: to me it is very natural that reviewers react totally differently to the same things. I believe it hardly ever happens that they all agree. Also, from one night to the next you can dance a role quite differently. So perhaps one night I'm seen in a brittle performance and then perhaps another night I was a heavy performer; I don't know. But it can be very different. So I don't necessarily think it is so amazing that reviewers write different things. Indeed, you sometimes think they are not writing about the same piece. But they are; yet they get such different impacts from it. I think, Jerry, what you say about qualities is important; at least it is important to a number of us in modern dance. Maybe to us it is more important than anything else. But a lot of people find it hard to see. There are a lot of dancers who don't see it. Because you can come out of certain schools without having ever heard of quality, because for them it is sufficient to look just at the facts.

SIEGEL: I'd like to say something about this "brittle" thing. I think it has a pejorative quality in some people's minds when it is just dropped onto you like that. I was using it in a larger context. I was using it thinking about an opposition between two personalities and not about any particular performance. I was trying to work with a question that came into my mind. Who were these two dancers? Why did they work so well together? What did they have that complemented each other? If I thought this would someday be an issue I probably wouldn't ever have used the word.

GREENE: Although I agree with Jerry that perception and conception can't be separated, I don't want anyone to sit in the ballet and say, "What do I think about that? How does my philosophy apply?" In my particular philosophy I use the term "bracket out," or I talk about putting the things I know or the things I heard or the things I read into parenthesis so I can watch just as Marcia described.

But at the same time I can't undo everything I have learned. I put it aside at the moment and later I draw on these resources I hope I have accumulated, and somehow what I have known may be altered that little bit because of what I experienced when I set what I knew aside. But I wanted to make clear to my friends here that it never occurs to me that someone should watch the ballet analytically or reflectively. I think you do have to open yourself up. In the same way I don't think you should go to the museum and keep talking all the time or identifying the painting in history. I think in many ways we do agree. I think Jerry should have a chance to respond.

MYERS: When I talk about presuppositions I don't mean necessarily ones that are consciously being entertained at the time. I don't mean one is necessarily watching the dance with a great deal of mental interference. But I think Marcia may be underestimating the amount of background or experience she is presupposing when she watches a dance. And when you compare the way in which a Marcia Siegel's eye is looking at the dance with somebody's who has not seen very much dance, there is a great deal of difference. What I am saying is the difference lies not just in the act of seeing, considered as a virtual turning off the mind, but in a seeing which is being guided by a tremendous amount of mind that has accumulated over past experience.

When I ask the question, why would many of my friends, people unaccustomed to dance, not understand a typical review, say, by Deborah Jowitt?, I think an important part of the answer is they are not accustomed to looking at dance in the way she does. So I ask myself, what is it dancers and critics, those close to art, those who understand and appreciate it, what is it they see that the untutored eye doesn't? I come up with the conclusion (based, of course, on many years of discussion with dancers) that it is something that for the ordinary person is relatively elusive—namely, movement quality. Then I ask myself, what is this movement quality? Is it an afterimage? Is it an illusion? Is it some sort of subjective response? I note that if we told Lucas the movement qualities he was striving so hard to get were just things in our heads, then he would be depressed.

SIEGEL: No one said they were in your head. Who said it was in your head?

MYERS: I believe that is one suggestion that comes with the idea that what you are really reviewing are afterimages. But, more importantly, where else can such qualities be, if the most acute eyes of the most acute critics disagree about their presence "out there" in the world or on the stage?

GREENE: I'm troubled about the idea of afterimages as something in your head. Is it possible to say that when you look at the dance you are conscious of it at a certain moment, you are perceiving it, you are looking at its qualities, but when you are sitting at the typewriter you are conscious of those qualities in the dimension of memory? But that's different from saying the qualities are in your head. You are addressing yourself, it seems to me, to your engagement with the phenomenon but at a different point in time. I get upset at the idea of something in your head, somehow cut off from something in the world.

MYERS: But you wouldn't really think the afterimage is anywhere else? I mean, if it's anywhere, I suppose it's in your head. I want to note further that if you say that when you are sitting at your typewriter writing a dance review, and are working over your afterimages, what you are trying to do is match up the afterimages with the actual performance, then you must admit to having your mind or eye somehow on the performance and not just on the afterimages; otherwise you wouldn't know in the least what you are trying to match up with what.

DEBORAH JOWITT (in audience): I have a problem with that. I understand philosophers are accustomed to thinking of issues that would drive a working critic absolutely bananas. Of course I am constantly dealing with memory and the relation of memory to the actuality. That's useful speculation for you, but if you show me a photograph of your son, I say he looks like a handsome kid. I don't say, "Jerry, I realize this isn't your son. It's just a photograph of your son." We don't have to deal with each other that way. So I think we have problems thinking along those lines, although I understand what you are doing.

And I also object to the kinds of qualities you mention, as if they were all the same kind of qualities, because I think some of them are very different from others. Most of the ones you mentioned were nouns and sometimes adjectives and adverbs. I think certain verbs imply a quality. I think "trudge" implies certain qualities. But a quality like lightness, which is one you mentioned, I think, in connection with Gelsey Kirkland, is one of those qualities a lot of us can agree about. We don't argue when a feather falls whether that is light or heavy. We accept certain things about lightness. Now the review you quoted used "saccharine." Saccharine is not the same category of quality lightness is, and that implies all sorts of associations and value judgments. So it is not right for us to sit here and talk about all qualities as if they were the same. Or defining "brittle," which I accept perfectly well as a stylistic attribute of Lucas at one time or another and not at all pejorative. But I don't want to define Lucas by that. That's just one word.

MYERS: I didn't for a moment think Marcia was trying to sum up Lucas with that word. I simply took it as an example of what I thought was a basic interest, of both dancer and critic, to do some finely-tuned looking in order to detect qualities of movement such as "light," "airy," "brittle," "tough," "tight," "restrained," and so on. I certainly agree with you, Deborah, that there are different types of qualities. But I thought that was too ambitious and complicated to get into tonight.

However, I don't mean to be playing philosophical games here. If I have a photograph of my son, yes, we can say it is a good photograph because you can match it up with him. The suggestion here, though, is that if you are dealing always with afterimages you can never really match them up with the performance because it is forever gone. And that leads to a view which I think is "loaded." It can encourage a critic to defend her writing on the grounds that it is all basically subjective, all she is doing or can do is to report very faithfully what remains as memory images. I don't think that is enough. I think the qualities, if they are indeed essential to what the choreographer and the dancer have done, are objective properties of that performance, but then it becomes strange why we don't all see them.

JOWITT: I think that is what I meant in saying a quality like lightness is an objective quality and saccharinity is extremely subjective, and that is perhaps the distinction between the kinds of qualities.

MYERS: Saccharine is perhaps suggested by another quality of the movement. It may be a higher-level characterization. But, in any event, I submit the critics ought to be impressed by the fact that so far as the newcomer to the art is concerned, they are giving fine-tuned descriptions in referring to qualities, and that's where the action is, so it becomes very interesting to decide what the status of those qualities is. I think it is unfortunate to drift into the "philosophical" view that qualities are just illusions, just things going on in one's responses. That doesn't do justice to the dancer, the choreographer or the performance.

GREENE: I acknowledge what you say, but the thing that should concern us is how to find ways of moving people to look in such a way that they can respond to qualities. The trouble is they respond to jumps and they respond to enactments. So whether or not qualities are objective, what really interests me is what kind of language can one find to move people's attention towards them rather than towards just the spectacular jumps. What can you do to make people see qualities? I'm as much interested in that as I am in the objective character of them.

SIEGEL: I have never said I am describing illusions. And I don't know good critics who are writing about illusions or think they are writing about illusions or want to write about illusions. They are writing about the dance, however you want to move it around word-wise.

MYERS: The danger is not that the critic will actually say in a review that movement qualities are subjective or illusions or only exist in the viewer's responses. But it is very easy, I think, to drift into the views that either these qualities are terribly elusive things out there or, on the other hand, that they are just things in the eye of the beholder. Neither view seems to me satisfactory. I think the qualities of movement which we convey by words like "light," "airy," and so on are reasonably elusive qualities. But you are only going to see them the way the critic does if you understand dance the way the critic does; not necessarily consciously analyzing while you are watching, but if you appreciate the dance, as Maxine was saying, over and above the circus and athletic feats, and begin to get that finer-tuned viewing, then you've got something fascinating going on. It is very important to the dance, to the appreciation of the dance, to the criticism of the dance, and to the communication to the non-dancer.

SENTA DRIVER (in audience): It seems to me you have a remarkable confusion between memory, which I think you must disapprove of, and hallucination. It seems to me you are suggesting that people who describe things in ways that differ from how other people describe them must have been making them up and that is why you object to them and ascribe them to be in someone's mind. They are in the memory. Do you have some objection to memory?

MYERS: I do think it is strange to say what the reviewer is reviewing is her or his memories. I would think what they are reviewing as best they can remember is the performance itself.

SIEGEL: What does that mean? Reviewing memories? I am not reviewing memories. I am writing an article about what I saw.

MYERS: Then there is no reason to call it afterimages.

SIEGEL: I didn't call it afterimages, but it doesn't matter what you call it. I just said what I am doing.

TOM WARTENBERG (in audience): It seems to me the discussion has gotten a little sidetracked by worrying about whether what the critics are reviewing is a performance or a subjective memory. Really, as I understand it, what Jerry was doing—and maybe because I am a philospher I know the language he talks a little bit better—is to worry about the status of critical claims. What he is saying, and I think that is sort of opposed to things you said, Marcia, is that when the critics say something they are saying something that is either true or false, and that when other critics say something, that is also either true or false, and there can be conflicts and one of them is right and one of them is wrong. That view is very different from the view that sees critical claims as a personal expression of how a dance moved you or something like that. Maybe, if there is room for a discussion it should be more about the status of critical claims and whether what you are doing is trying to talk about your experience of a performance or trying to say something about the performance that is either true or false.

SIEGEL: Well, I said at the very beginning I don't think any of it is absolute. Dance is not an absolute. It is not a true thing or a false thing, so how can we who are trying to make contact with that art write about it as if it were an absolute? I would never attempt to do that, and I wouldn't want that responsibility and, besides, I change my mind sometimes.

MYERS: I don't think anything I've said bears upon the question of absolutes, relativity or anything of that kind. If I say there is a packet of Lifesavers here, that this statement is true, I don't need to talk about absolutes. Now, if I read in a review that a certain dancer is fantastic because of her airy, light, restrained movement, then I do assume, yes, Tom is right, the critic thinks she is making a true statement, just as when I say there are some Lifesavers here. But I don't think it has anything to do with absolutes.

AUDIENCE: I want to go back to Marcia's earlier point about going to a performance and maintaining as much openness as possible and trying to view that performance without any particular preconceived notions. I'm a little concerned with the implication that any of us can attempt to be a blank slate as we view a dance performance. Your past experiences as a critic, as a human being, as a dancer, whatever, have formed a conceptual framework into which you place those experiences and you sift those experiences out into those that move you and those that don't move you. Some things in the performance you will remember; some things you won't remember. Everyone who goes to a dance concert sees different things, whether or not they have the educated eye we talked about last night. I am wondering if the power of the critic may somehow negate the past experience and the conceptual framework another spectator may attempt to place upon that dance performance. People are very afraid to go against the experts and may think, "That was wrong. I felt that but really shouldn't have felt that," when really it was your past experience being very different from their past experience.

SIEGEL: There are so many ways to answer that question. One way is to talk about who gives me the power. I think I'm pretty out front about my preconceptions. I try to know what they are and I try to tell people what they are. I try to be in touch with what I distinctly don't like and why. I think we are not engaged in flattening everything out so that everybody is alike. We're engaging in just the opposite. I have a sense of who I am as a critic. I try to tell people what that is and I expect my reader to have a sense of who I am as a person. If an audience or a reader is beset by some kind of thing called the power of the critic. I am not asking you to give me that. I am not asking you to follow me slavishly. I would like for you to disagree with me. I would like there to be many critics who write intelligent, differing views of things. I would like there to be *less* power of critics, and I personally don't identify with those critics who write into their own power. But I'm not interested in being accessible to everyone. I'm not interested in making dance seem wonderful. It's not interesting to me to write that way. If it were, perhaps I would be an historian or something else. I write to satisfy myself, to answer a challenge in myself that the dance puts to me. A question, a response, a dilemma, a satisfaction—those are things that dance provokes in me, things I choose to pursue intellectually after I have seen the dance. And I do that through writing. This has nothing to do with some kind of objective mush about what everybody likes. I just don't think that's what I'm supposed to do or what you're supposed to do with it.

AUDIENCE: I have a few reactions to what Mr. Myers said. The only way to see the quality is not by reading something by the critic, which can only open a small door, but by a long-term exposure and commitment of some sort. And I think the other danger in what you are doing is applying an academic perspective to art. I think that's dangerous because we are dealing with subjectivity and not facts. You were talking about facts before, and a performance is not a fact. Good art isn't about facts. When you look at something, when you look at a dance piece, at a painting or a sculpture, ideally it will create a reaction within you that will be different for all of us, and it's not a fact. It's a personal fact, but it's not a universal fact.

MYERS: I think you and I are actually in agreement about the requirement of a certain kind of experience or education to become aware of these qualities which you and I apparently both agree are essential to the appreciation of dance. So I think we are together there.

You see, I mean my remarks to be a testimonial to the very important function which the critic serves. I'm not in any way taking an adversarial position toward the role of the critic. I compliment critics such as Marcia and Deborah Jowitt and Arlene Croce. I compliment them on really being very close, it seems to me, to the hearts and the minds of the dancers. What they do, and I think in an admirable way, is to call our attention to what are at the hearts and minds of dancers—namely, qualities of movement.

Then I ask you to reflect on this singular fact, that these qualities which are so important and central to the art of dancing, can become so elusive to us. I can understand how one may prefer to exit the theater saying, "I don't care what anybody else sees; I'm just writing about my own response," and so on. But suppose, though, you backed up for a moment and said you really did care whether there was some sharing of seeing in that audience. Then it becomes an important question. What are those qualities that some people see and others don't?

SIEGEL: I'd like to say something about qualities. I've been wanting to because I do feel that's what I am trying to work with very much. But each time I have been about to bring it up we get into another one of these verbal traps. Jerry is putting all this into very strange language. He is bringing in words like "essential," "sharing the experience," and "caring." Why bring all that into it? The question we are concerned about is not about essentials or sharing experience or everybody perceiving the same thing or having to know something everyone else doesn't know. It's a question of discrimination, sophistication and getting deeper into a thing, and what I'm concerned about is what makes these different from each other.

Why did Lucas dance differently from José? What is it that makes Gelsey Kirkland special besides a lot of people putting out a lot of publicity about her? So I might talk about the way she does a step that four other dancers in the same choreography on other nights do differently. And that's what I consider to be quality. You can talk about it in very raw terms as Effort-Shape analysis does, trying to break down the basic essentials of underlying energy change. And they do it in very raw terms. I am certified in Effort-Shape, and that is my basic movement training and it's very useful to me. I've worked with that vocabulary and with those concepts. But I no longer see them as concepts or as so raw and so simple. I don't remember when I wrote that thing about Kirkland, but I think I wouldn't talk about lightness at this point with reference to her, because that just doesn't seem quite as subtle as what I might say about her. But it might involve some degrees of lightness combined with some other kinds of things.

I am constantly searching for more definitive ways of pinning down those personality things, those energy things, those ways of phrasing, those characteristic styles of dancing and choreographing that you could call quality. I think they are very evident and I think they are very real, and I think they're totally tied in with the actual movement itself. They're just as real as an arabesque, and what the critic does is to see them in more detail with finer discrimination, fine in the sense of fine tuning. But I don't believe I ever said, "Gelsey Kirkland is fascinating because . . . Go run and see her." I think I try to talk about what interests me and why.

MYERS: What you say is pretty much what I have been trying to convey, Marcia. So I think we probably are basically in agreement here. If there was one question I thought maybe tonight you didn't really tackle, it was the question, "Are these qualities elusive to seeing? And if so, why?"

Lucas last night said that fifty years ago he saw a movement that freaked him out, and then just recently Alison Chase in Pilobolus did this very same movement and it freaked him out again. I thought there must be some really very fine quality there that freaks Lucas out. And he said last night he couldn't explain it. So here is a professional dancer saying there is something there that just grabs his attention and yet he can't tell us about it. There is something there he sees that is so elusive and yet so marvelous, and I as a non-dancer am fascinated by this, and am just asking you dancers and critics to help me see it, too.

HOVING: See, I think it was not the movement, it was the quality. Quality is harder, maybe, to define in dance, but I believe as soon as you go to a concert everybody knows what quality is. One conductor interprets a symphony in one way and another in a very different way. It's a very ordinary thing. For me, it's normal that critics write differently about performances. But quality in dance . . . it's a newer thing; maybe people haven't lived as long with it. But surely most people recognize it in music. It is a very illuminating thing to go and hear an orchestra rehearse and what the conductor has to say about it. There are very few people in dance yet who work like that.

MYERS: That's right, and you can't just go and open your ears to a symphony, as Thurber couldn't just go and look in his microscope and see what's there. Something is required to inform that seeing, to find those qualities.

AUDIENCE: I'm confused by the discussion we had last night and by the discussion tonight. Last night we were talking about the role of the critic in guiding the spectator to see certain aspects of the dance, to increase the awareness of that dance. The critic can be very instrumental in the aesthetic education of the dance audience. Yet tonight you seem to have been saying you write on a very personal level, you don't write for everyone, you write for a specific audience, you hope your audience knows you or has somehow gained that knowledge from reading your reviews over time, and therefore to somehow understand the conceptual framework you place dance into and view dance from. When we are talking about aesthetic education and the role of the critic, it seems again we are back to the critic's powerful role as one of educator, leader, guide, helper. And I wonder if that's a valid role, whether you accept the diversity of a dance audience and the diversity of experience, whether the critic is actually able to provide those guideposts and to provide that aid.

SIEGEL: Maxine Greene is interested in education, aesthetic education, and that was the question being talked about last night. I'm not an educator when I'm writing. I do teach, but that's another hat. I don't think we get our education only in school. We're being educated all the time. We're learning through various kinds of experience, and I believe a free press and an intelligent press is one instrument of our education. I'm not the kind of teacher who says, "This is what's true and this is what I want you to learn." I'm perhaps egoistical enough to think my thoughts are interesting or possibly enlightening, or that somebody might want to find something in them, because I think things about dance that some other people may not think. But I'm not anxious that you should think what I think. I'm anxious that you should see a world of possibility. That's what dance is capable of, and that kind of response is one of the things dance is capable of inspiring in a person who is looking at it. I have a certain background, a certain amount of experience and a certain amount of training to give myself a better education than the average person who doesn't know anything about dance. So in that sense I think I am qualified to do what I am doing. People hire me to do what I am doing. The power thing I still say is in your mind. I'm not taking any responsibility for that. I'm taking responsibility to be a moral person as a writer.

MYERS: Well, I want to say I've certainly profited from reading Marcia Siegel's writings, which have helped me to understand, appreciate and see qualities of movement I probably would not have witnessed otherwise. And so I'm grateful to her, as I'm grateful to other critics who have helped me to see not only the choreography and the other things that are going on, but also what seem so important, these things called qualities of movement. As Marcia seeks to illuminate her experience, so this evening I've been trying to illuminate my experience in thinking about these things critics and dancers have helped me to appreciate and to respond to.

AFTERWORD TO GERALD MYERS PRESENTATION
by Marcia B. Siegel

Far from effecting a rapprochement between the disciplines of philosophy and criticism, this discussion, I think, widened the gap still further.

The philosopher assumes there is only one thing to see: the Truth. The critic knows there are as many ways of seeing as there are spectators, and each eye reports a different version of the same event.

Is there such a thing as objective reporting? Of anything? Even science, it appears, must change its definitions as new ways of observing and perceiving phenomena are discovered. And if we could report an art event "as it really is," would we want to?

Would a critic's "report" of a dance be of any more use to a reader than a detailed program note, an interview with the choreographer, a blurb from the publicity office or the stage manager's cue sheet?

I think most critics speak to the *experience* of art, not to its mundane manifestations. It is in fact the very lack of specificity underlying all art, the many-sidedness, and the appeal to what is most personal in us—including our mind, memory and feelings—that constitutes art's irresistible, inexhaustible lure for the critic.

I think Gerald Myers mistakes the act of criticism for reporting, and misreads Arlene Croce's "afterimage as subject" statement to be a confirmation of this error.

I do not equate words with facts. To me they are of a different order of reality. A dance may be a certain thing, a fact. But the words I choose to reflect that dance can come from many possible ideas, can be fitted together in various ways, and even once set down can resonate differently for different readers.

I view words as dynamic, volatile and undependable. I don't endow them with fixed meanings if I can help it. I don't think the writer's search for precision represents some deadly act of taking aim, through which she hopes to impale the truth forever. I don't wish to take upon myself the job of passing judgment or issuing the ultimate label. The idea that I might permanently stigmatize another person in one word is repellent to me. Nor am I engaging in combat or dispensing praise, blame or favors.

In constantly speaking as if that were what critics do, Myers made it impossible to deal with the real methods of our craft, which he initially termed notorious—possibly in jest.

Myers reinforces all the public's cliché fears about critics. He insists that we provide the reader with crutches, with definitions to prop up his doubts and insecurity. But why must the critic, unlike all other witnesses to a dance, be infallible? Myers invests us with powers we don't seek, and then wants us to defend a position we haven't taken.

Perhaps he is groping toward an account of the perceptual process: how does a viewer take in and recognize an event? But this process is still entirely mysterious to me, nor do I consider it within my professional competence—or function—to understand it. What I do strive to understand, and to elaborate on in the most effective language, is what I perceive when I'm looking at a dance.

For the past ten years I have studied the observation of human movement, and I continue to train my eye, my memory and my kinaesthetic awareness. I consider myself a qualified observer. While I take this skill to be the first obvious requirement for a good dance critic, Gerald Myers questions the very existence of such a skill.

Through his own spectacular wordplay, Myers not only refuses to let the critic play anything but a frightening, repressive role *vis-à-vis* dancers, but denies the skills and intuitive resources that are so essential if critics are to be more humane.

Much to the discomfort of myself and Lucas Hoving, he lifted a few sentences out of the context of my work, as though they were the only, the absolute record of something he took me to be describing. Then he wanted to test these words for their validity, to probe the sincerity, the accuracy, the competence with which they were arrived at.

Had I known in advance that I was going to be challenged in this manner, or had I read Myers' extensive—and I think incorrect—dissection of the way we identify movement qualities, I could have chosen appropriate examples of my writing that would illuminate my process of perceiving and verbalizing, or I could have shown film to demonstrate my approach. But to justify a premise falsely set up (that is, the word "brittle" as a sole definitive characterization of a dancer) would have been to acquiesce in his distortion.

RESPONSE TO MARCIA SIEGEL'S AFTERWORD
by Gerald Myers

When Marcia Siegel suggests that what my paper seeks is an understanding of the perceptual process whereby we recognize movement qualities, she understands me correctly. Like her, I find the whole of that process difficult to analyze. But, in noting how movement qualities can seem elusive and how critics can differ about them, I offer the explanation that seeing such qualities depends in part upon one's perceptual training or education. I then argue that to say this does not commit one to a "subjectivist" account of movement qualities. Since I emphasize throughout my high regard for the perceptual skills of professional critics, and since I choose passages from Ms. Siegel's writings which strike me as both exhibiting those skills and illustrating what movement qualities are, I remain puzzled as to why she finds only thorns in the bouquets that my paper extends to the critics. At no point does my presentation presume to question the soundness of any critic's specific judgment about a dance or dancer. It does note that critics and dancers do differ in their perceptions of movement qualities, and this reminds one of certain philosophical questions that are asked about the nature of "seeing." These questions are relevant, but in a totally friendly way, to the philosophical task of determining what is missing when we don't see, or what is present when we do see, the same movement qualities which the critic sees.

About the Appreciation of Dance

Presented by Paul Ziff

I AM GOING TO TALK ABOUT problems about the appreciation of dance. These problems are problems I think for one who is concerned to view a dance as a work of art and to appreciate what is being viewed. I don't think they are insurmountable problems but I do think they pose genuine difficulties in the appreciation and evaluation of dance and I think these difficulties are then difficulties in forming aesthetic judgments about dance and difficulties in forming any kind of sensible aesthetic evaluation of the whole process. The first thing I think I want to say is that though many people are inclined to say dance is a language that's really an unfortunate way of thinking. If you think of dance as a language then you may be inclined to approach it to attempt to appreciate it in the way one appreciates a language to attempt to understand it in the way that one understands a language and that just cannot be. It is not a language. I will go on to suggest to you that it may well be thought of I don't know how strictly but it can certainly sensibly be modeled in terms of a symbolic system. But not every symbolic system is a language. I can give you a simple example. All of you can use road maps I trust in one way or another. In order to use a road map you have to read a symbolic system: red lines black lines distances and the like. Again you can understand the use of code flags and the like. In all these cases one is dealing with symbolic systems but not with a language. Now I'll have to be a bit more technical and I'll use some technical terms to explain more precisely to you why dance is not a language and what kind of symbolic system it can be thought of how it can be modeled in terms of symbolic systems. But don't be worried by the technical terminology because I'll explain it. I do like to put things precisely and then to slop around a bit afterwards. So long as I have said it precisely I don't mind the sloppiness.

Speaking precisely then the reason dance cannot be a language is that it lacks the appropriate syntactic and semantic structures requisite for a language. It has syntactic and semantic structures adequate for a symbolic system but not for a language. More precisely still dance lacks in the most general form either metatheoretic or concatenative or recursive structures. Now let me explain that.

Metatheoretic structures are exemplified in the ordinary use of language in a very simple way. We use words to talk about words. I can say the word "dog" is spelled with a "d." In so doing I am using the word "dog" to talk about the word "dog." That's something that's quite characteristic of language. It occurs in some communications systems; for example crows will caw about cawing so they have a minimal metatheoretic structure there but they do it to a very limited extent. A papa crow will teach a baby crow to caw in the right way. So in that sense they have something of it.

The second aspect of language that's essential for linguistic structure is concatenation. We join words to words to form phrases compounds sentences discourses. You can talk of something being red; you can talk of an apple; you can talk of a red apple. Or a more peculiar structure: you can talk of something that's oil: you can talk of a lamp; you can talk of an oil lamp. A red apple is an apple that's red. An oil lamp isn't a lamp that's oil; it's one that uses oil. It's a different structure.

Concatenation doesn't really occur in any interesting way apart from genuine linguistic structures but there are some examples of concatenation in dance. Movements can be joined to movements to form sequences of movements so you have at that level something of the aspect of concatenation. You find the same thing by the way in bird calls. Herring gulls have an attention call and an alarm call and they put the two together and you have a compound call which functions as a compound call.

The third essential aspect of a language is what's called recursive structure. Indeed this is the most significant part of linguistic development apart from concatenation. Recursive structure can be explained fairly simply. In technical terms a function is recursive if it takes as an argument to the function its own value. Putting it in simple terms if I say something like "It is raining" I can then take that sentence make it into a subject of a sentence and say something about it. I can say "That it is raining is true." And then I can take that sentence and make it into a subject and say "That that it's raining is true is absurd." What I have said is in fact quite correct. It is not raining. What I have done is use a recursive linguistic structure to produce this complex utterance.

Again you find something like that in connection with animals. In bird song you find recursive structuring of a motif: the chaffinch will sing a motif which is embedded then in a more elaborate motif which is then embedded in a more elaborate motif. And in dance you can find something like that. There will be movements and then more complex movements embedding the repetition of the initial movements and perhaps then still more complex movements.

It is at the syntactic level that you find these things in connection with animals and animal communication and in connection with dance. Let me explain to you the difference between the syntactic and semantic level of a language or of a symbolic system because that's quite important in order really to understand what kind of symbolic system dance is. If one speaks of syntactic relations in a language one is talking of relations between words groups of words words to words so for example if I say "red apple" I use an adjective and a noun. That's a syntactic relation: the adjective operates on the noun. Syntactic relations relate certain formal elements to other formal elements. It's a patterning. In dance dance viewed as a syntactic system it's very clear that it has an elaborate syntactic structure. Let's consider what the elements of dance are from a syntactic point of view. This is leaving out all questions of meaning now. Just the elements that enter into a dance.

The most obvious thing one has of course to begin with would be the dancer. That is to say a moving object. The object is generally a person. It needn't be a person. It could be a robot for that matter but generally customarily it's a moving person. A person who is capable of various movements. Persons groups of persons are the central objects in dancing. But of course there are other objects. These are the objects that constitute the props around the person. They may be scenery chairs anything. There need be nothing of that sort but there may be.

Then there are the other objects which serve to define the space in which these movements take place: a cyclorama a stage prop of some kind a backdrop of some kind. They may or may not be these. There will be something that serves to define the space however. So we have essentially two kinds of objects to begin with: one the moving ones that we call the dancers the other the objects which surround the dancers and which serve to define the space in some way. And then the matter is complicated even further. There are two other elements of a radically different sort. Both of them or anyway at least one of them is absolutely essential to the dance and that is light. If there is no light and the dancers are dancing in say the Carlsbad Caverns without any light one is not going to have much to appreciate. One may get some auditory phenomena but that's about it. So one has light and the light can of course be enormously varied spotlights floodlights any kind of light and all kinds of patterns. They could be stable or not.

And then in addition to light of course there is sound. That's the other fundamental factor. The sound can be music it can be agitando the sound of the flamenco dancers' heels whatever one likes but there is sound. So we have sound light objects in a defined space well or poorly defined. (I am not for a moment suggesting the space has to be well defined.) These provide the syntactic basis for a dance. Still speaking now at the syntactic level what one has is change a change in these configurations. The dancers will move in one way or another. I toyed with this idea for a while: Could you really say you had dance if you simply had immobile persons on stage who did nothing and only the lights moved? If you had the lights flashing back and forth which could indeed create the appearance of movement? I think you might say it was a dance of lights but it wouldn't be a dance in the ordinary sense in which we speak of a dance. And if nothing moved not even the lights then I don't think it could be said to be a dance: or if it's a dance it's a limiting case of a dance.

The syntax of dance poses enormous problems. These now are not problems of appreciation but I'll digress for a moment to mention them. What's the relevant difference between different changes of this configuration the configuration of persons dancers the objects the lights and the sounds? Say we have some change. What's the difference between those changes of the configuration we are presented with which constitute the performance of a dance and those which do not? I mean suppose we got a bunch of people up on the stage just sort of staggering around. I don't mean staggering around the way a dancer would stagger. I mean just sort of walking around or shuffling about the way a crowd will shuffle about. Presumably one would say if that's a dance it's a very bad dance but how does one draw the line between what counts as a dance and what doesn't? With respect to that I'm afraid I can say nothing illuminating because I haven't the foggiest idea how to draw that line. I think I could have drawn that line fifty years ago. Then it wouldn't have been too hard because all kinds of movements were ruled out.

One has an analogous problem in connection with works of art in a gallery. What constitutes a work of art? This at one time wasn't very hard to say. One would say a statue or a painting something like that. I recall going into a gallery not too long ago and tripping over a bunch of potatoes on the floor and I said "What is that?" and somebody said "You have tripped over my work." If that's a work of art and I'm not joking I'm not saying it isn't then I don't see how to draw the line between what constitutes dance and what doesn't. I think you do get to a limiting case if you have absolute stillness no change in configuration. But apart from that I don't see how to do it.

You might say there ought to be a way of doing it and I sympathize with the feeling but I don't see how to do it. Anything I think of about the movement like the movement has to be interesting and expressive can always be countered by saying you simply haven't cultivated a taste for this kind of movement. Let me give you an analogy. It used to be thought that if you could say something was boring and evoked nausea then that couldn't be a work of art but many many works are designed to be exactly that: to be boring or to evoke nausea. And some of them are profoundly interesting in the way they do do this. Some of Andy Warhol's movies are profoundly boring. I am thinking of one about a kiss that lasted for I don't know how long.

73

That's one of the problems that occurs in connection with syntax but that's not a problem of appreciation: that's more a problem of I suppose creation. Where can one draw the creative line? How does one say this is and that isn't a dance? But the syntax of dance does pose an enormous problem for the audience. If we are concerned with moving persons moving objects of any kind a change of configuration which depends upon light and sound and the relation between these moving objects and the backdrop in the defined space then where you see it from is an enormous problem because clearly if you sit on one side of the auditorium viewing this space and I sit on another side we do not see the same thing. It will be quite a different configuration.

You can say this is also true of a piece of sculpture but the thing about a piece of sculpture is you can walk around and come back to the original spot. When one views dance ordinarily one has a given position in the theatre and one cannot really walk around the orchestra pit changing seats constantly. Anyway if you did you would be missing a lot of the show. So one is stuck with a very limited perspective. It's extremely difficult to see ballet in fact to see modern dance to see any dance unless you're in a very privileged position you are the only person in a very small space and the dancer is dancing for you. Then you might see just about everything. But with any ordinary presentation in theater if you are high up you see one thing if you are low down you see another. Lateral movements can become invisible from certain places. Certain patterns which are visible from overhead are not visible from below. A choreographer may be inclined to draw a bunch of scribbly lines for the dancers going across the stage. That the lines are scribbly will only seem so from some perspectives. From others they will take on totally different shapes.

Now you might say that if you have sufficient knowledge of the dance knowledge of the tradition and so forth regardless of where you are you can take in what the movements are. I have thought about that and I don't believe it. I started to reflect on what the topological problems would be. This would mean visualizing a moving line in space and trying to determine in a three-dimensional space from one position exactly what the trajectory was or think of them as vectors forces moving in space which probably would be more accurate: there is no way absolutely no way you can visualize this particularly if the dance pattern is novel unfamiliar. You simply cannot capture all of this. You might say the same is true isn't it of watching any sort of theater art: you don't see everything.

There is another difficulty of appreciation. Now still at the syntactic level I haven't moved to the semantic problems yet the difficulty is this: with a play you see certain things from certain sides of the stage but you can do something with a play that you cannot do with dance. For one thing you can read the play in advance. You can't do that with a dance there is no way. Secondly you can see it again. Whether or not you are seeing the same play again is fairly easy to determine. I don't see how I can give you any strict criteria. That's another matter. That's rather hard to do. But nonetheless one can be fairly precise about this and say yes this is the same play no doubt not being performed in exactly the same way it's a different sort of rendition but still it's the same play. How does one show this? One takes the script. The script will show it. It's the same thing going on. So you can see *Julius Caesar* in modern dress. It's the same play though a radically different interpretation. So one can identify the play on the basis of the script and identify different interpretations of it.

When one turns to dance there's no way in which one can do precisely that because there is no script like that. There are notes by the choreographer: these may be fairly good there may be a notation of some type that will be pretty good but this doesn't even begin to capture all the other things going on: the lighting the sound and the particulars of the arrangements the particular movements that take place at that time. One thinks yes this is an interpretation of the dance and we know what the dance is. I don't doubt that in some sense we do but I don't really see how we can pin it down nor do I know how we can become very precise about this. So to put the point very simply I don't know how you know that you see the same dance twice whereas I do have a better idea about how you know you see the same play twice. The fundamental difference is that with the play there are fairly explicit stage directions and there is a very explicit script and there isn't anything as explicit as that in connection with dance.

Maybe someday there will be some splendid notation devised which will govern everything and if that were so then this problem could be alleviated. It still would not alleviate the problem of the person trying to see what's happening the problem of which perspective to view it from.

Now I'm not suggesting this makes it impossible to enjoy the dance you see but I do think this makes it extremely difficult to give any kind of critical evaluation of what you see because it may be you have chosen a particularly bad spot in which to view the ballet or the dance.

Quite possibly from one perspective it's rather poor and from another it is not. Contrast this by the way with what you do in listening to a piece of music. There is an acoustical character to halls to music halls such that if you have a good one it really doesn't matter where you sit—oh within certain limits it will if you have an abominable seat behind a pillar which echoes or something like that. But go to something like the Academy of Music in Philadelphia almost all the seats are good seats and you can hear pretty much the same piece of music. The same would not be true for example if you were listening to something in the Church of St. Marks in Venice when say there is a performance of brass choirs by Giovanni Gabrieli. There it's very important that you sit at exactly a certain place because Gabrieli used the resonance of that church in a very special way. The brass choirs would echo and the reverberations would come to a certain point and if you are at that point you can hear what he wanted you to hear. If you are not you won't. So you can't possibly take just any seat there. But in most acoustical works it's relatively indifferent where you sit. That's not true not at all true with dance. It is relatively indifferent where you sit in connection with a motion picture. If you sit too close to the screen there will be enormous distortion for a short time but your eyes compensate for this owing perhaps to all kinds of Gestalt features of perception.

These are difficulties in forming a critical evaluation of a dance: the difficulty of viewing the same work twice and the difficulty of making sure you had a reasonable perspective on it. Much of what the choreographer did may be invisible to you if you have a bad seat.

I think much more complex difficulties occur at the semantic level of this type of symbolic system. To speak of semantics in connection with any kind of symbolic system is to speak of a connection between the syntactic elements the objects the words or anything that constitute the system and something else which can be said to be that which these entities mean or that which they serve to express and the like. So for example if I say the word "dog" is used to refer to a four-legged canine I'm telling you something of semantic import about that word. I'm telling you what that word is used to refer to.

Or if I told you the word "perhaps" means the same as the word "maybe" I'm telling you they are virtually semantically equivalent. They are not strictly semantically equivalent because although they have exactly the same meaning they don't have exactly the same tone. The connotation or suggestion of "maybe" is slightly lower class than "perhaps." You can find this out by doing field research in linguistics. So I like to give talks in which I say "Maybe I'll do this and perhaps I won't." But that's the only difference between those two. So I'm telling you something about their meaning.

When one turns to a symbolic system like that of dance what one finds is not that the principal elements in all this namely the motions of the dance or if you like the changes in the configuration before you have a more general meaning nor that these particular configurations or motions have any specific meaning. They may on occasion. There are trivial cases where one can get something like a straightforward propositional meaning a statement of some sort. In pantomime one can say "Yes he is saying his dog is over in the corner." Or there may be a kind of story associated with it. There may be a written program with it. You can then associate the written program with the details of the story with the gestures of the dance. But generally there is nothing like that which is not to say the elements of the dance are devoid of any semantic value. Quite the contrary: they have a much more interesting semantic value than that. On occasion they have that trivially but what they genuinely have is expressive character. The movements of a dancer can be profoundly expressive. I needn't remind you of how expressive movements can be. Take the most trivial thing a threatening gesture. You can see this as threatening. You can feel it as threatening. There are all kinds of movements that are expressive.

I said to you that though dance may have something of a recursive structure from a syntactic point of view that is syntactically speaking the elements are woven around other elements and all of them woven around others: at the semantic level there is no recursive structuring. If you have some gesture which is expressive and another gesture which expresses something quite different you cannot just put the two together and get the result to express what the earlier two expressed individually. You can't say take a word like "oil" and a word like "lamp" each of which has meaning put them together and then get the meaning of "oil lamp" and then you cannot say "That there is an oil lamp is interesting" and "That that

77

there is an oil lamp is interesting isn't at all interesting." You can't make that kind of move.

The meaning of complex movements the significance of complex movements in dance is not a simple function of the meaning of its constituents. It doesn't build up recursively in the way linguistic elements build up.

What kind of meaning what kind of significance do these movements have? How is it to be characterized? If you think of dance as a language which is the thesis I am inveighing against then you would be inclined to say that if these movements are part of a language they then must mean something and if they mean something we should be able to say what they mean and if we can't say what they mean then something is wrong here. Because if they do mean something if it is linguistic why can't you say it? I mean there is no such thing as one natural language which completely fails to communicate what some other language will communicate in one way or another. I don't mean to say what can be said in one language can exactly be said in another. That is not true. But certainly one can get something of what is said. You can approximate it in varous ways. But there is no way of saying what is expressed by a movement in dance that will express it to the extent or can capture it in the way it's expressed in the dance.

This makes it sound very mysterious. That's because you tend to think of it as a language. So let me give you some analogies here to try to characterize what kind of expression is involved. I say movement in dance is remarkably expressive and indeed many dancers and many choreographers seem to be primarily concerned with it. I was reading an account by José Limón of what he wanted to do in a dance and how he would approach a certain topic and everything he said pointed in this direction: the movements had to be profoundly expressive. He characterized what they were supposed to express in very abstract terms. But he didn't try to say what each movement was supposed to do even though he thought it very important that each movement be terribly expressive.

Let me give you an analogy. If one looks at certain objects like a mountain or a mountain range one can see these mountains as impressive as powerful as awesome as brooding as having all sorts of characteristics. Psychologists particularly Gestalt psychologists here speak of physiognomic characteristics: characteristics of objects which serve to evoke certain feelings certain emotions certain attitudes.

I'll give you a very nice example. Somewhere around Phoenix or Tucson there is a rather famous range of mountains called the Superstition Mountains. When I was down there I wanted to go and see them and I tried to find out where they were. Someone told me just to drive down the road and there will be several mountain ranges and then I would come to the Superstition Mountains. And I said "How will I know I'm at the Superstition Mountains? I mean how do I tell these from any other mountain ranges because there is just one range after another?" And they said "Don't worry about it when you get there you'll know it." So I drove and when I got there I knew it because they were impressive they were awe-inspiring. You could see why these would be mountains that would be sacred to the Indians whereas the other mountain ranges didn't have these characteristics at all.

What did I see? Strictly speaking I saw a certain configuration of rocks and the like and there's nothing I could say about this configuration of rocks that would really clue you in to what makes them so awe-inspiring. They were very tall but so were lots of the other mountains. They were kind of jagged. I'm inclined to say they looked lonely but when I say that I'm already moving to its expressive character and not telling you anything strictly about its physical form.

Let me give you another example. Most of us can read the expressions on other people's faces particularly in our own culture. If it's not our own culture that's quite another matter but intracultural expressions aren't all that difficult to read. If somebody comes up to me and has a threatening look looks hostile looks angry I know it. Generally I know it not invariably you can be mistaken sometimes. There is a good friend of mine a philosopher who has an angry look. He was born with an angry look. You look at his face and you would swear he's angry. But I know him and I know that's not an angry look. That's just the configuration of his face. But if an ordinary person had that look on his face you would say "Yes he's got an angry look."

We can all do this. How do we do it? Never mind that for a moment. Let me give you another example. This is a famous example. I got this from the late John Austin a philosopher at Oxford. It was one of his favorite cases. Someone in England designed a teapot that had a marvelous spout that would in fact not drip. Not a single drop would fall off that tea spout. It would pour into the cup and leave no residue. But when you looked at the spout you would swear the thing would drip. It had a drippy look. As a result no one would buy it. They would say that thing has got to drip and you can't pour tea from it. It had a rounded spout I mean a big thick spout and you would just swear the water would drip all over the place. So no one would buy the teapot. Why? Because they quite rightly said it had a drippy look and if it has a drippy look then most likely it would drip. In this case it wouldn't.

Another case another one of Austin's. He was shown through a prison and he turned around and looked at one fellow and said "He looks like a criminal." And someone said to him "That's the warden." Whereupon Austin replied "Well he has a criminal look anyway." Which is quite right. One can recognize certain looks as having a certain character as expressing certain attitudes as displaying certain attitudes. How is this done? I think unfortunately unfortunately for the sake of dance critics the people who like to write about dance and particularly with respect to the expressive aspects semantic aspects of dance I think most likely the answer is there is no analysis of this available. That there may well be even from a perfectly solid theoretic point of view no way of analyzing those features of a face which make it an angry-looking face a cheerful-looking face no features of a mountain which will enable you to analyze it as being awesome morbid brooding and so forth. The idea that there must be an analysis of these complex features seems to me simply naive. I'm not saying you can't mention salient features. If you want to mention a sad face and tell someone how to draw a sad face you say turn the mouth down draw someone's mouth so that it curves down. A happy face draw the lips curving up the way you do clown faces. That's easy to do. But all of us know we can see a clown with his mouth drawn up looking very very sad and there is no way you are going to say the salient features determine inevitably what's going to happen. You can have any of those features and still not get the expression or you can get the expression without any of those features.

I can't prove this but I can give you a fairly simple case: strictly speaking it's not simple but it seems to be. If you start to draw on a blackboard just with a little chalk—if there were a blackboard here I would draw you some of these—shapes and configurations of dots and configurations of lines and so forth such that you can say you see a triangle then how many different kinds can you form and what would be the analysis of the situation such that you could get a computer to identify each one of these as a triangular shape?

As far as I know there is no known theoretic solution to this. The ways of determining whether something is a triangular shape do not admit of analysis.

The late John von Neumann one of the great mathematicians and essentially the creator of the modern computer discussed this problem once the problem of what he called visual analogies. He pointed out that if we take seriously the devices the physiological devices and mechanisms available to human beings which enable them to identify something as triangular it must be a system as complex as a computer with 10 billion relays because one is using approximately one-fifth of the human brain which is the visual cortex. You have in each one of your eyes approximately 100 million receptors. If you think of the complex network that would be required to simulate this to get a computer to do what a human being can do the computer would today have to be something of the size of Texas: it would be a gigantic machine. We are nowhere near that yet. All these people who talk cheerfully about robots walking down the street next week are just perfectly silly. We may get a robot walking down the street I mean the kind you see in kids' movies but you are not going to get anything that will do what human beings can do not in the area of visual perception not for a very long time. I don't mean to say it's impossible. It's just technologically unfeasible at the present and probably not feasible for the next 100 years.

The complexity of the analysis that people are capable of using the visual cortex for is really staggering. In consequence we are able to identify things as sad gloomy morbid friendly and so forth. We can feel and react to expressive characteristics and gestures even though we cannot spell out how we do this: we can do this of course in various in very many areas. All of you know perfectly well what a table is or a chair is but I doubt any of you can define the word "table" such that it will give a correct specification of all and only those objects you are prepared to call "a table."

You can use lots of words without being able to say what these words mean even though you know what they mean. But just so you can recognize and appreciate the expressive aspects or movements of the dancers' movements without being capable of any analysis. Does this mean the critic is in a hopeless position? The person who tries to analyze what's going on he's in a hopeless position? Yes and no. If the aim is to analyze the expression in a dance thoroughly completely then you might as well forget about it. Go home. It can't be done.

If the aim is to make clear to others one of the interesting and salient features of the expressive movements performed in the dance then the person who is concerned to criticize the dance from that point of view can be of great help. What one needs is a very very sensitive human being who can perceive these things who is thoroughly familiar with the dance so familiar that he or she can see what he or she in fact does not literally see appreciate the character of the movement going on on stage and thus overcome the difficulties posed by the syntactic aspects of this symbolic system.

Someone sensitive to the expressive aspects of the dance can serve to make it clear to others. Such a person can help others notice things they didn't notice and attend to things they didn't attend to. And for that reason I think we need someone we need very good critics very good analyses of what's going on in the dance. All I'm suggesting is you mustn't suppose there should be anything like a complete analysis and you mustn't look for or you will just be bemusing yourself you mustn't look for anything like the kind of analysis you might get with an actual language.

This kind of symbolic system most likely will permanently resist analysis. Let me give you one analogy here. It's fairly easy in books on harmony and on contrapuntal technique to identify what's fairly good harmony and what's fairly unusual or bad harmony. It's not too hard when one deals with the vertical component in music the harmonic structure to detail it and give guidelines for it.

It is I think virtually impossible to give any adequate guidelines for the melodic structure of music. If someone asks "What makes a melody a melody?" I think there is no good answer to that and how do you find out whether something is a melody? There's only one way: you try it on a sensitive ear a sensitive human ear. It's quite possible and there are very good theoretic reasons for thinking this might well be so that there is no analysis possible of what constitutes a melody. A melody may be like what's called a book code something that cannot be cracked in any way unless you have the book and it could be a melody is a melody because something uniquely structured in the human brain is roused by it. There need be no other explanation.

I think the same may well be true of the expressive movements in ballet and dance generally. There need be no good reason why these movements are expressive save that human beings are innately structured to respond to them. On the other hand there may be some movements such that some analysis is possible particularly if it is not innately determined that they be so expressive. And critics can be of great help there. Persons concerned to analyze the dance may indeed come up with something very useful.

So I suggest these are the difficulties one has to attend to in trying to appreciate dance and I think for that reason one could say dance is vastly more interesting than a language. It calls for extreme sensitivity close attention and of course there are all sorts of aspects of the dance I haven't even alluded to. But this alone would make it something worthy of attention because it's difficult and being difficult is something very good in connection with art because you don't quickly get tired of it.

DISCUSSION FOLLOWING
PAUL ZIFF PRESENTATION

Panelists: Noël Carroll, Deborah Jowitt,
Senta Driver, Paul Ziff

NOËL CARROLL: I think it is a very provocative paper and I really have no basic disagreement with it, only a few small points of disagreement. I am very happy with his observation that dance is not a language. I teach and write in the field of film where the idea that film is a language is one of the most pernicious metaphors, and, though I'm not sure many people are pushing the idea that dance is a language, there is nothing like a preemptive strike early on and I fully agree with that.

First I'd like to talk about the problems he brings up in regard to syntax. I think Paul is assessing the problem of visibility from the perspective of a viewer who is basically unfamiliar with dance. I don't mean Paul himself is unfamiliar with dance, but he is adopting that perspective in his approach to the problem. The unfamiliar viewer is confronted with a world of motion and it is impossible for him to see everything or to know where to look. But part of what it is to see the performance is to know one is not supposed to see everything. Dance and theatrical performances are institutionalized in certain ways. They have genres, they have conventions. Perhaps "rules" is too strong a word, but there are conventions of viewing and those conventions of viewing make the necessity to see everything and to attend to all of the changes in lighting and the problem of one's seat beside the point. Ballets have been created in the tradition of a proscenium stage. What's relevant in the ballet is what is viewable, except in some theaters with particularly unctuous and rapacious managers who have put the seats behind pillars. What's there to be seen in the ballet in terms of the institutional presuppositions of the performance of ballet is what's viewable from any angle. Now, it is true, as Paul points out, that everyone doesn't see the same thing. But people in some sense of the word comprehend or apprehend the same thing. There are categories of shapes, categories of composition in choreography that the person who views ballet has at his or her disposal, and these give a kind of foreknowledge. That is, not everything in that world of movement is relevant. Some of the things that are relevant we know from having seen other ballets, from reading about ballets and from taking ballet classes.

What I'm trying to get at is that I don't know the rules of cricket and when I see a cricket game I more or less experience what Paul describes. I mean, I experience that world of confusion. Cricket viewers, apprised of the rules, know what is relevant to see. They know that there are no particularly privileged seats, that the cricket game is made for the whole cricket audience.

What I'm trying to suggest is that we have historical knowledge about these dance institutions, and those help us to choose what's relevant in the syntax to look at. Though it is true in a certain physiological sense that we don't all see the same thing, yet we all do perceive the same thing, at least if we share these conventions.

I'll just make some quick remarks about Paul's observations on semantics. I think he's right, we're in dire straits about getting the kind of analysis of physiognomic form he suggests we might require. But I wonder if we need so powerful a kind of analysis; I'm not sure we need a physiological analysis. Some of the techniques by which expression is achieved in dance seem to me to have a kind of logic, not a formal logic, of course, but they seem to rely on certain characteristics we could describe as we describe reasoning patterns.

For instance, it seems a lot of expressive effects in dance depend on our ability to perform reasoning in terms of homologies. In our culture we have realms of terms, color terms, sound terms, and we are able to interanimate them so that we say dark correlates to sadness, which correlates to slowness. I'm not saying homology alone will explain all the types of expressive devices one finds in dance, but there are aspects of the conveying of expression in dance that may have kinds of subtending structures that can be quasi-rationally reconstructed and it's not just a matter of homology. For example, in the Limón concert last night, you could see a whole range of ways in which expression is made in those dances. First of all, simply through narrative. That is, the Othello character in *The Moor's Pavane* can be seen as expressing sizes through the normal kind of inferential system we use in narrative in general. Most of us know Othello anyway, but we also infer the anger at a certain point in the dance, not just simply on the basis of the gesture itself but the way it fits in with all the other narrative assumptions we have made all along.

There are obviously a large number of techniques for instilling expressive effects. I'll just mention one more, one Freud mentions in his descriptive rather than theoretical writings. This is a technique that's highly parasitic on language. It's rather like charades. Freud describes it as dramatization. A word or a gesture or an image can evoke a word in our minds, and this is not exactly pantomime. It's not structured in terms of a set of rules, but within a certain given context a gesture as in a game of charades can evoke an idea. There is a good example in Limón's *Carlotta;* it occurs when Maximilian is dead and all of Carlotta's handmaidens are ransacking the palace and stealing the crown. One way we know how little they think of her is that a pair of them run out and as they run out they leave her flat on the floor in her red gown. It happens so quickly that all you see are two women rushing from the stage and then suddenly Carlotta is flat on the floor. Now what immediately comes to mind is the idea that they ran over her. What I'm trying to get at is that we have a range of devices for instilling expression. I'm not satisfied to leave it all at physiognomic features. Undeniably there is some expression that is the result of physiognomic features. All I want to suggest is that there are other devices.

DEBORAH JOWITT: I've never really worried about dance as a language either. I have no quarrel with that at all. It never occurred to me. I think they are separate kinds of symbolic systems with their own rules, art and language. But in my job, I am not really concerned with making definitive analyses or aesthetic judgments. I think perhaps I have to see my job a little more pragmatically to accomplish anything at all. The question about what a dance is is something that passes through my brain but none of the parameters mentioned can really work for me. I have seen dances in the dark—you will please take the word "seen" on another level—that is, I have been at dances in which there was no lighting, and I only heard the sound of the dance. I have been at dances where dancers were immobile for the entire dance, and I have been at dances where ordinary people shuffled about for the duration of the dance, and I was able to accept them all or deal with them as dance. I think in a sense, perhaps, there is a way dance reflects upon itself. I think some of those dances were statements about previous statements in dance, about dances of a preceding generation, or dances that took into account an audience that could make reference to another kind of dance form that had preceded it in time.

I would also say I think there is a slight bias here in favor of words. I don't think I can see the same dance twice. I don't think I can even see the same dance once. But I don't think I can see the same play once, or twice either, regardless of the fact that it has the sacred words of its text written down, and that we tend to accept those words readily, as "the play." It may dismay anyone in love with words to consider how the Royal Danish Ballet has passed down many of Bournonville's ballets from the 1830s to the present. Ballet masters and dancers, taking some notes, remembering in their bodies the teaching of their predecessors, hand the steps along. It's obvious that, watching *La Sylphide* or *A Folk Tale*, I could not say for certain I was seeing those "same" ballets. I'm thinking now of all the many *Moor's Pavanes* I've seen. What is *The Moor's Pavane*? Where is it? I don't know. I don't think it is only the performance I'm watching, and I don't think it is the notation score. I'd make, of course, convenient assessments, perhaps in terms of original performances. I think of Lucas Hoving and I think perhaps he is Iago for all time, for me, and everybody else stands or falls in those terms. I could do that. Perhaps I do. And yet I'm willing, on some perhaps insane level, to accept the fact that here I am writing and being paid to write about something I never see the same way twice, that I am prepared to say can never be the same. I'm prepared to say I don't even know what it is when it isn't the same and yet I write about it. How do I do that? Perhaps because I take the view that what I will write about is what I am seeing myself in however bad a seat I have. And I deal with that in relation to whatever ideal versions I think might exist. I think I can tell you, if it's necessary, what constitutes a threatening gesture for me in a particular context, but in order to do that, I wouldn't analyze only and all those gestures I am prepared to call threatening in order to tell you why a particular one is threatening. And I think there are traps in thinking there is any perfect vantage point.

Paul Ziff speaks of Gabrieli. You sit in a certain place in the church, you hear what Gabrieli wanted you to hear. I understand there is an aurally optimal place where you can hear the balance of the choirs, but although Gabrieli may have known the church, he didn't know my ears. And therefore, I would never have the hubris to suggest what I could see in a dance is what Limón wanted me to see, but only that, with whatever soul and eyes behind a pillar I have. I try to conscientiously account for what I see at that particular time. Noël spoke of knowing and not knowing the rules of cricket. In dance I guess I learned the rules by watching the game, and that's what I'm used to doing, and so my process has to differ very much, or I would really have to leave the field and find some other way to make a living.

SENTA DRIVER: That's all right; you don't have to do that. I'm not going to leave the field, although I found this very enlightening as a person who is preparing two new works, one of which is called *Body Languages* and one of which is called *Grammar*. Stay tuned.

I don't know quite what to make of this. I find a lot of what Mr. Ziff says very persuasive. I still think there isn't quite so much of a problem seeing things as he seems to think. The bumblebee can't fly but it does. It may be, as Noël says, that we are using too precise a rule, that too exhaustive an analysis is wanted. It isn't necessary. Everyone thinks they are seeing the piece. The people who think they are seeing only a part of it are either screaming at the management or they are sitting in front of *Private Domain* by Paul Taylor, in which case they are not supposed to see the whole thing. We have even had pieces in which you are not supposed to be able to see the piece. Anything is possible.

I think it's fairly recent that choreographers have become interested in using the word "language" or "system" about their work. It still attracts me and I'm still looking for what I am going to do. I am in love with words and I make work also. I still think it's possible. But the burden is on us to prove, by example, that it is. We probably are talking about syntactic systems without realizing it. We are talking about grammars, we are talking about what symbolic logic calls, I think, or did when I was studying it, perfect languages, small perfect languages. I cherish a notion that you can devise a movement system or set of habits, if you will, and use it to prove something as scientists use experiments to prove notions or to discover notions or to demonstrate facts or to create facts. We can't know whether that's possible until I show you or until someone shows you. Words do not need to be so far removed from the work that is done on the stage under the title of dance. I get restive when I hear it said that it's the critic that does the thinking about dance and it is the person who writes for a living who is wrestling with words or not wrestling with words or reducing things to words when they shouldn't, because I do these things and I am not a critic or in any of the usual roles of writing about dance.

We all can think about dance, not just the people who write. Probably much of the reason why we have used the word "language" is we thought it would give us respectability. But it may lead somewhere. Many of the people, I think, who are interested in the weak notion of dance as a language or their dance as a language, may not be interested in semantics in the first place, may not be interested in meaning anyway. You don't have to care about meaning or expressiveness. You don't have to be in the business Limón was in or using the assumptions I believe Limón was using, to be interested in the transmission of information, to be interested in making suggestions. These aren't very perfect words, but I think there is a difference between meaning as José may have understood it and as dramatic choreographers may have understood it, or the creation of emotional situations and something which is not simply a demonstration of A plus B, this move plus that move, but a demonstration that adds up to something. I think Noël will have something to say about this tomorrow.

It was a convenient word, "language." It meant something to ordinary people, ourselves included. That's why we used it. I think your points are well taken; it's not a complete word, but it gave some of us a new direction to go in, considering the history of topics choreographers had used. If you think it is a language, even if you are wrong, you may focus on not just what you say but how you say it. I have believed it is possible to perform in the subjunctive mood. That may only be possible in some medium like television, but it may be possible also in live performance. Anyway, without the notion of language you can't get to notions like that. It wouldn't occur to you. If it's simply a crutch for our creative thinking, that's another issue.

I have nothing much more to say about this except that I have to think about it. I may have a long summer of work ahead of me, but I appreciate the point. I just don't think the problems of our seeing things together, as my colleagues have said, are so great. People do manage to do what they do, manage to go away and all argue about something and believe they are talking about substantially the same thing. It does happen, and should happen. The television camera can't see everything, but the human eye does. As you said, robots can't do it but people are extraordinary. We needn't talk about the worst possible case or the worst possible seat. I don't know if that's a complete answer, or an answer, but it's a response.

PAUL ZIFF: Well, I'd like to say something first about Noël's remarks. I largely agree with what he said. I think one can do all the things he says one can do, but there is one point I find extremely difficult. What I was suggesting was that the syntax of dance poses an enormous problem for perception on the part of the viewer. He rightly points out that there is some sense in which you seated in one part of the auditorium and I seated in another can rightly say we have seen the same dance, even though what met our eyes was in fact quite different. The movements you were able to observe were not the ones I was able to observe. That's certainly true. But what I was pointing out was the uniqueness of this situation in dance. It's quite unlike any other art form, and the justification, insofar as there could be one for the claim that we do see the same, is going to be enormously difficult. If you and I look at an apple, you stand on one side and I on another, we can certainly say we see the same object. The reason we can is because the visual aspects of the apple are not important. When we say we see the same apple, we are concerned to locate an object in space and it's that thing before us. That you happen to see one aspect of it, namely, its front side and I see its back side, makes no difference.

But with works of art, particularly the kind we view, one is inclined to think generally, and this is true in virtually all the other arts, that the visual aspect you attend to is extremely important. If you look at a painting at one side and one distance, and I look at the same painting at quite another distance, there is a very good sense in which we have not seen the same thing and we are not prepared to enter into any critical discussion about this, nor can we compare our appreciation. You must come look where I have looked and I must go look where you have looked. These are quite different things. The visual aspects of a painting are important. You can't ignore them. The thing is a visual object primarily. That's what you attend to. Now, the striking thing about dance is that on the one hand it seems to be a visual object—well, visual and auditory, of course. I'm ignoring the auditory features. Yet, we somehow have to transcend the differences in our perceptions. Now, Noël rightly points out that an historical perspective on the dance and thorough familiarity with the dance form will enable you to do this. If you are quite familiar with the dance then, and I'm quite familiar and we have the same background, yes, we can say we have seen the same thing, but this is precisely the difficulty I was pointing to. How is this done? It's all very well to say it's the historical knowledge that informs you. I quite agree. That's probably the way it's going to be done, but how does it do it? Noël says we have this apprehension with historical knowledge. Well and good. Explain it to me. How does this apprehension come about? And when you view the thing very strictly as a topological problem, it seems to be enormous. You must have such a familiarity with this dance, it seems to me you must have seen it from every perspective, just about. And then you recall it. And if that's so, then we never do in fact view the same dance.

But other than that, I quite agree with everything he said. I think the homologies he pointed to are useful. Dark, sad, slow—these things all go together, but that wasn't any problem either. My problem was, why do dark and sad and slow go together? Why is sad slow? Why isn't sad very quick? And sometimes it can be. Well, there, you say, there's a correlation of some sort. Maybe it's behavioral, and so forth. I think, ultimately, one comes back to physiognomic characteristics, so I think they are more important than he is suggesting here. I think these homologies generally rest on them. However, I don't really disagree with what he said because you can do precisely what he said we can do.

With respect to Ms. Jowitt's remarks, I do object. I object strenuously. You cannot see a ballet in the dark—I mean pitch dark.

JOWITT: Why?

ZIFF: Because in order to see anything you need radiation, flux of lighting impinging on the cornea, etc. What you can do is to visualize, but to visualize is not to see. You are quite mistaken if you think there is no difference; there is a profound difference. I can imagine things; I can visualize things. That's not seeing.

GERALD MYERS: Paul, there is a question from the audience.

AUDIENCE: I see a dance critic or writer, any critic of any art form, as a creative individual in his or her own right and the success or failure of a dance critic is his or her ability to use language, which is no less perfect than movement or music or whatever, to relay in some way the essence of what the art is, and if critics can choose their language sensitively, they can perhaps give someone who was not in the theater the essence or feeling or idea of a response to a work of art that is in some way understandable to the person reading it. I would like to also say I think you can see a dance in the dark, if that's what the choreographer intended you to see. I've worked a lot with music and I would bet you $50,000 that the finest musicians in the world, put into that Italian church playing the Gabrieli piece, would probably sound quite different, because I think concepts of tempo have changed from the first time a half note was put on a staff. So I think the imperfect relayer of information is language and it is constantly attempting to relay what is perfect, which is what has happened here.

ZIFF: Well, I'm afraid there's one profound difference between us with respect to the use of words. You like to speak metaphorically. I do not. I repeat, you cannot see something in the dark; you can visualize it. I don't see any necessity to speak so fancifully. I don't care what the designer of the dance intended; he is not going to get me to see anything in the dark.

Secondly, I can see darkness, but darkness is not a dance and you don't see darkness really. Have you ever been in Carlsbad Caverns when they turn out the lights? It's a splendid experience. You can't see your finger in front of your eyes. With respect to languages, I think you are quite mistaken in saying a language is somehow imperfect. I have no idea of what notion of perfection you can invoke to make sense out of that. It's true the expressive powers of languages differ. If I say, "La vita e la vita," in Italian and translate it as "life is life" in English, it doesn't come across. "La vita e la vita" is ever so much more expressive. But I can easily not express but communicate, in English, what is expressed in Italian. That is, I can describe it for you. I cannot create the same effect but I can tell you what was said. It says "life is life" and it has a profound tone and suggests all kinds of things, and we could spell this out. There is quite a difference between the expressive and the communicative powers of language. There is very little difference in the communicative power between civilized languages. It's a dogma of linguists which I don't subscribe to, but it is virtually universally held that all languages are equal in communicative power. I don't believe that. But I'm probably the only philosopher of language who denies that. But virtually everyone agrees they are not equal in expressive power. The nuances of one language are not expressed readily in another, which is not to say they cannot be communicated. They can be described but not expressed. It's like telling you what the joke is and telling you a joke which makes you laugh. If I can explain the joke it doesn't mean you wouldn't laugh at it. There's a difference between telling a joke to make people laugh and saying what the joke is, describing it in a boring way.

Now with regard to the other point about language being an imperfect vehicle for the expression of what is expressed by the dance, I think that is a very bad way to look at things. It is not at all an imperfect vehicle for that. It's not a vehicle for it at all. It's rather that these expressive characteristics are very subtle; they call for sensitive people. I am not for a moment suggesting critics like Ms. Jowitt should be out of business. On the contrary, I am saying they are absolutely essential. They are sensitive to what's going on and they make clear to others, insofar as they can, what to attend to and what the expressive characteristics are. I just suggest they are not going to analyze anything in great detail, but that's not very important. It's not very easy to analyze what makes a Klee painting so powerful or so mysterious. But one can draw people's eyes to the work and enlighten their viewing of it and that's what the critics do.

DRIVER: The only response I would want to make is that you do have to put yourself in the hands of the people who make the work you wish to consider. You may not think it's very good, but you have to take into account the fact that we control, imperfectly or perfectly, the thing we are presenting. If we are stupid about it, it won't get across. If I make something I intend you to perceive and experience without movement, without floor, without sound, without living bodies or without any of the other thousands of things dancers have removed, that is what you are given; you cannot wish it to be different. You can wish it to be different, but you cannot make it different. It is not different. The piece does not exist when the lights are turned on if it's intended to be done in the dark. I have seen that piece you are referring to, but unfortunately I have only seen it with the lights on. I wish I had experienced it in performance.

JOWITT: "Experience" is perhaps a more accurate word if we are worried about whether "see" is objectionable.

DRIVER: You can disapprove of these things, but as you said yourself, you were not going to draw the line at stating what would constitute a dance, which is a wise thing to do because we have been having at that ever since the notion arose. That is a red flag to us. Anything they say isn't a dance we are going to go and try to disprove.

ZIFF: I wouldn't object to your saying you experienced the dance any more than I would object to your saying you could experience a concert. I once attended a concert where the violinists were instructed to keep their bow one inch above the strings and they played the whole work that way. Their fingers moved, but there was not a sound to be heard. I don't think I would say I heard that concert. I attended that concert.

DRIVER: You can't, however, complain that you were in a bad seat for that particular piece. There is just no way, and Sol Hurok is not going to give you your money back.

ZIFF: Good example. You have just refuted one point I made. I had thought there was no way people all could experience the same dance but I had not thought of the dance in the dark and, clearly, there is no privileged seat for that.

DRIVER: Unfortunately, you also haven't thought of some of the work of, for example, Merce Cunningham, who hopes you will at least rush about or sit in every possible different seat. There are more ways of experiencing some of this work than sitting in the best seat. If I make a work for the seat in Row G, then that's the best seat, but if I don't make it that way then you can't claim there's a problem between you and any other viewer.

ZIFF: No, you are right there too. I certainly didn't mean to rule out that somebody could design a work like that. I don't think you can rule out anything when it comes to what people are going to do.

DRIVER: So many of us do. An awkward habit we have.

Post-Modern Dance and Expression

Presented by
Noël Carroll

PHILOSOPHERS AND DANCE THEORISTS like
Selma Jeanne Cohen[1] and Monroe Beardsley[2] have used the concept
of expression as a central ingredient in their definitions of artistic
dance. For example, Prof. Beardsley says of a movement that

> If . . . there is more zest, vigor, fluency, expansiveness or stateliness
> than it appears necessary for its practical purposes, there is an overflow
> or superfluity of expressiveness to mark it as belonging to the domain of
> dance.[3]

From certain perspectives, dance just can't help being expressive
because the human body (it is argued) is intrinsically expressive;
philosopher Joseph Margolis explicitly assumes such a position
when he claims a dance cannot be identified by a choreographic
score of the sort that Labanotation affords.[4] Margolis holds there are
expressive attributes of the original performance (and performers)

95

of any dance that are, so to speak, embedded in the performers' bodies, which will not show up in any enumeration of the movements of the dance no matter how precise the notational system is.

Though expressiveness is taken as a *sine qua non* of dance by many academic theoreticians and critics, there is also a movement afoot on the part of many post-modern choreographers[5] to create works that are non-expressive or even anti-expressive.

Corresponding to post-World War II developments in painting and sculpture, these choreographers—my example will be Yvonne Rainer—attempt to compose dances that are neither representational or expressive, that is, neither referring to nor suggesting events or emotions, fictions or feelings. These dances are meant to show nothing above and beyond the specific movements employed in making the given dance.

Frank Stella said of his paintings that "what you see is what you see,"[6] that is, lines and color (in the paintings that have color). Analogously, some of the most interesting post-modern dancers have designed works in which what the spectator sees is movement as such—movement putatively shorn of representational or expressive import.

Like other revolutions in the history of art—especially those of the twentieth century—this tendency in dance is connected with a philosophic outlook on the nature of the (dance) medium. The position is reductionist. It conceives of dance as movement *per se*. It regards the formal and expressive inventions of ballet and modern dance as vestiges of "illusionism." Polemically, such vestiges are designated as excrescences that "disguise" movement in terms of shapes or emotions.

Thus, we are confronted with two conflicting positions. On the one hand, there are theories that dance is expressive, while on the other hand, there is a choreographic practice committed to non-expressive dancing.

Several interesting questions arise from this apparent loggerhead that are pertinent not only for dance theory but for criticism and choreography as well, namely:

1. What is it these avant-garde choreographers have achieved and how have they achieved it?
2. Have they successfully created non-expressive dances?
3. What can be learned of the relation of dance to expression as a result of their experiments?

Answering these questions isn't easy for a number of reasons—not the least of which is the vagueness of the concept of expression. Among other vexations, the kinds of things we are willing to say get expressed in the arts are heterogeneous and unstable.

In the narrowest sense of expression, popularized undoubtedly by artistic movements like Romanticism and Expressionism, we say what gets expressed in art are feelings. In dance, for example, we say a movement or a phrase or an entire piece of choreography metaphorically possesses a kind of emotional attribute we normally ascribe to people. In the performance of José Limón's *Carlotta* the other evening, the dance opens with Carlotta (Carla Maxwell) shrouded in a bluish-gray cloak, illuminated by a milky spotlight. She pulls and tugs on the fabric in a way that is reminiscent of Martha Graham's *Lamentation*. The tugging plus the lighting cause sharp diagonal furrows to streak across the surface of the "costume." We associate the pulling and the tense diagonals with inner turmoil. We do not say Carla Maxwell in *Carlotta* and Martha Graham in *Lamentation* are literally buffeted by inner turmoil, but their movement metaphorically has the quality of inner turmoil. Other candidates for what gets expressed in art in general and dance in particular include joy, anguish, terror, ambivalence, etc. For an example of ambivalence, consider last evening's performance of Limón's *The Moor's Pavane*. Othello hears Iago's insinuations and essays a high, powerful kick, turning then in the direction of Desdemona with plaintive gestures. This series of gestures expresses his emotional vacillation toward her, swinging between anger and tenderness, between belief and disbelief.

But we also ascribe other than emotive labels to dance movements. These encompass a more inclusive range of anthropomorphic qualities, adding to the emotive labels ones that refer to human vices and virtues, modes of bearing, personality traits, attitudes and ways of being-in-the-world. These anthropomorphic qualities—like wit, charm, majesty, aloofness, sentimentality, generosity—are often attributed to dances whose choreography is said to metaphorically possess and project them.

For example, in Steve Paxton's *Satisfying Lover* anywhere between thirty and eighty-four performers walk across, sit or stand on a stage according to a score.[7] The piece can be executed by non-dancers. It abets the play of comparison and contrast on the part of the audience since it provides a wide assortment of body and personality types engaged in the most mundane actions. As you can imagine, the dance, in contra-distinction to the feats and virtuosity of ballet, has an extremely casual air about it, a mood quite appropriate for the late Sixties when it was made. Many of the performers were anything but casual; many were nervous. But the piece as a whole can be metaphorically seen as casual.

We can see some choreography as expressing personality traits not only of individuals but also of human groups. In Balanchine's *Serenade*, for example, the innovative use of the corps and the concomitant de-emphasis of principal dancers in the choreography—in opposition to the practices of classical ballet—give a democratic tone to the dance. Writing of the end of the first movement of *Serenade*, Marcia Siegel states that

> Just before resuming their first formation, the entire group does a fast circle of piqué turns around the stage. Again I have the idea that Balanchine is suggesting some new idea of egalitarianism. Piqué turns are a showy, applause-getting device usually performed by the ballerina at the end of a pas de deux. Yet Balanchine says all these dancers can do it.[8]

We can easily see the structure of reasoning implicit in Siegel's analysis. She pinpoints a deviation from the balletic tradition. She evaluates the deviation not only as a subversion of a technique but also as a rejection of the values associated with the technique. She derives the expressive quality of the choreography, in this case egalitarianism, by postulating the contrary of the value, in this case hierarchy, associated with the subverted technique.

In the narrower senses of expression, what gets expressed is either an emotion, or some other anthropomorphic quality. But there is also a broader sense of expression, one that is very close to the notion of communication. In this sense, ideas as well as feelings and other anthropomorphic qualities are what get expressed. Kurt Jooss' *The Green Table* wordlessly states that the shenanigans of plutocrats cause wars whose wages are paid by the common people. Such dances not only suggest anthropomorphic qualities but in a loose sense also imply certain propositions by means of inducing the audience to infer the propositional commitment of the dance as the best explanation of the choreographic and/or dramatic choices in the work.

I've introduced these somewhat rough distinctions between different senses of expression not in order to propose a perfect cartography of the concept of expression but to provide some tools for unearthing what post-modern choreographers have and have not achieved. I think they have drained expression from their choreography in the narrowest sense of expression, that is, the expression of feelings, but certainly not in the broadest sense, that is, the expression of ideas. Whether they have drained their dances of the possibility of being legitimately appreciated in terms of anthropomorphic qualities other than emotive ones is a more nettlesome question but one whose answer I think hinges on the fact that their dances are expressive in the broadest sense of the concept.

In order to get a handle on these issues, let's consider a concrete case—Yvonne Rainer's *Trio A*. Made in 1966, it is a four-and-one-half-minute dance originally done as three simultaneous solos by Rainer, Steven Paxton and David Gordon at Judson Church in Greenwich Village, New York. At the time, it was entitled *The Mind Is A Muscle, Part I*. In subsequent works by Rainer the dance reappeared again and again in all sorts of variations—as a solo, a duo, etc.[9]

What is immediately striking about the dance is all the features it lacks *vis-à-vis* more traditional balletic and modern dances. There are no arresting gestural shapes—neither frozen moments nor movements like *pirouettes* or *jetés* that evoke a sense of an abstract, choreographic geometry or "Gestalt." There is nothing resembling Humphrey's symmetries or asymmetries that give poses and movements a readily perceptible, easily remembered "pictorial" structure. The gestures are often small and busy, not easily assimilated in terms of large formal designs of the sort that a choreographer like Yuri Grigorovich uses to structure movement.

Related to the lack of arresting gesture, no special parts of the body—like the extensions—are privileged. Head, hands and legs all move, not only defying the idea of a balletic line, but also making it difficult to summarize the style in terms of a part of the body as one might with the Limón style in terms of emphasis on the upper torso.

The movement does not shape or articulate the performance space by drawing circles or lines across the floor. Contrast this with Limón's *Choreographic Offering*, which we saw last night. In the opening of that piece, the dancers constantly reorganize the space by means of different, repeating geometric figures, for example, a circle with two arcs partially surrounding it. But in *Trio A*, the body is merely a moving point in space. That movement does not suggest a floor plan that the spectator can use to evolve a sense of structure or a set of expectations about the trajectory of the dance. As a result, the spectator encounters difficulties in perceiving the dance, that is, in knowing how to look at it, as well as in remembering it.

There are no repetitions or variations of movement phrases. Again think of *Choreographic Offering* with its carefully sequenced phrases; the audience learns to anticipate that a gesture by one group of dancers will be echoed shortly afterwards by another group. But in *Trio A,* the phrases are independent modules. A unit of skipping precedes one of kneeling that precedes one of flipping over that precedes one of what might be called torso rippling. These units are difficult to see (comprehend and remember) not only because they don't refer to any standard dance movement vocabulary, but also because they are never repeated so as to give us the opportunity to become familiar with them.

Moreover, there is no demarcation between the phrases; each seamlessly blends into the next. And, in terms of tempo, there are no climaxes in the phrasing, just a constant pulse of what is meant to look like an even expenditure of energy. These stylistic choices involve a rejection of several choreographic means for temporally organizing movement. There is no development or variation. No step grows from an earlier one as an echo (for example, *Choreographic Offering*) or as a variation (e.g., Humphrey's *Passacaglia*). There are no climaxes or pauses. *Trio A* thereby eschews the ebb and flow rhythm important in much modern dance. Just as the dance has no Gestalt in space (in terms of gesture or composition), it frustrates conventional expectations of a "shape" in time.

There is no story, character, attitude or action that the movement can be correlated to; thus, *Trio A* forgoes all the traditional narrative devices for enhancing the perceptibility and memorability of the movement. The dance is difficult to perform, but a non-dancer can be trained to do it. Hence, it lacks virtuosity in terms of the typical denotation of that term.

The total effect of the stylistic lacks or denials cited above is to make the dance particularly hard for the spectator to see in the sense of perceiving it under some overarching temporal, spatial and/or expressive concept. The spectator is compelled to attend to the movement as such. *Trio A* is very difficult to remember because it is very difficult to categorize (and store) in light of our customary ways of looking at dance. As a result, it has a kind of "presence," that is, it must be perceived on a moment-to-moment basis; it cannot be referred to a spatial/temporal design, an image or a feeling. Each phrase, each movement module is its own set of motions, neither repeating or portending others nor suggesting a coherent play of emotions. In the vocabulary of Nelson Goodman, *Trio A* could be called an attempt at exemplifying movement as such, that is, it is presented as a sample of movement possibilities divested of any of the wonted dramatic, theatrical, expressive or formal designs that characterically structure dance.

Trio A denies expressive effects in the sense that none of the movement is metaphorically emotive but it is clearly expressive in the broadest sense; it is discursive—it calls attention to hitherto unexplored, even suppressed, movement possibilities of the dance medium. And it does this in ways that correspond to a recognizable interpretation of the dance medium.

In turn, the interpretation of the dance medium implied by *Trio A* reflects the aesthetic values of the art world from which it emerged. It is an attempt to collapse the distinction between Art and the Real that one finds rampant in the Happenings and sculptures (that is, Robert Morris) of the Sixties. Just as Minimalists revolted against Abstract Expressionists, striving to remove all the expressive traces and marks of the artist from their canvases, so Rainer revolts against modern dance, especially the Graham tradition, by denuding dance of emotive references as well as climactic phrasing. Rainer's goal is to present movement pure and simple.

Throughout the Sixties and continuing today, many artists seem to metaphorically model their activity on that of scientists. They often regard representation and expression as a physicist conceives of ordinary objects like desks and chairs. Artists "search" for the basic constituents or the "reality" of their media, like scientists searching for the building blocks of matter. Thus, we encounter paintings that are "about" color and line, or "about" flatness. These are proposed under the banner of anti-illusionism. In *Trio A,* Rainer situates the actuality of dance in movement. But, of course, this is not Real Movement in the sense of everyday movement. The movement in *Trio A* is rigorously and self-consciously designed and polemically charged. It functions as a highly discursive repudiation of very specific forms of dance as well as of the values associated with those practices.

We understand the discursive implications of *Trio A* in the same way we often identify expression in dance solidly within the balletic and/or modern traditions. Consider the earlier example of *Serenade.*

Siegel began by isolating a deviation from standard practice in terms of the handling of the corps versus emphasis on principles in classical ballet. The traditional practice had a culturally entrenched, associated value (hierarchy) which led Siegel to correlate a contrary value (democracy) with the deviation. Traditional practice offers a repertory of choices of technique: Both a list of available techniques as well as the possibilities of negating any one of those existing techniques by deviating from the available forms. This matrix provides the background against which we view new dances. The choices, conscious or intuitive, the choreographer makes are assessed as formal repetitions, amplifications or repudiations of existing forms of dance. In this sense, each dance is sedimented with dance history. A dance is seen as a choice *vis-à-vis* a tradition and as a response to it. Many dances, perhaps most dances, merely repeat the forms of preceding dance, and thereby implicitly endorse prevailing presuppositions about dance. With *Trio A*, Rainer could say "no" to the range of expressive (emotive) qualities that flourished in Graham and ballet. But *Trio A* is expressive in the broad sense, since, by systematically deviating from specific techniques, it leads us to infer that it is aligned with an alternate, contrary, anti-illusionist position on the nature of dance versus the "illusionism" of Graham and most of the balletic and modern tradition. Because of the historically-sedimented nature of each dance, it is hard to imagine how an avant-gardist could fail to be expressive in the discursive sense insofar as each deviation from tradition will imply (if only negative) some conception of dance.

In pointing to the historicity of dance, I am not referring to some mystical notion, but to something inculcated, as it were, in the very bones of dancers. Dancers are schooled in various techniques and in the process of that education they learn large parts of what I previously called "the repertory of traditional choices" as well as the values associated with the various techniques. When the dancers become choreographers, they can mine this vast reservoir of information intuitively. Often choreographers are more "eloquent" about their conception of dance in terms of the discursive implications of their work than they are verbally. Part of the role of the critic (or commentator) is to assess the relation of emerging work to the past, to say what is new and what is old in each work and to speculate on its implied significance in terms of our conceptions of dance. Since the existing techniques of dance have strongly associated values, it is a valid form of reasoning as regards dances to correlate repetitions or repudiations of a given technique with affirmations or rejections of the values associated with the technique. Consequently, we might agree that though *Trio A* denies expression in the narrowest sense, it does accrue broadly anthropomorphic qualities. In comparison with dances in the Graham tradition, its reductive choices make it "factual" as opposed to "emotive," "cool" as opposed to "impassioned," and "objective" as opposed to "subjective."

Notice that the way we project these anthropomorphic qualities is grounded in a very specific form of association. The projected qualities are relational, based on implicit contrasts between culturally entrenched contraries (for example, "objective" versus "subjective"). In attributing such expressive qualities to dance, we choose from a field of property concepts that are opposed to or contrasted with the anthropomorphic property or properties that correspond to a given subverted technique. As long as a technique has an associated anthropomorphic property, the subversion of the technique projects the opposite property. Thus, the historical character of dance plus the specific (contrastive) relational structure of the anthropomorphic metaphors associated with existing dance make it practically impossible for anything that is dance not to suggest some broadly anthropomorphic properties.

Editor's Note: The large number of references in this essay to dances by the Limón Company are direct allusions to a performance that occurred on the preceding evening.

NOTES

1. Selma Jeanne Cohen: "A Prolegomenon to an Aesthetics of Dance," in *Aesthetic Inquiry*, ed. M. Beardsley and H. Schueller (Belmont, Calif.: Dickenson Publishing Co., 1967), pp. 274-282.
2. Monroe Beardsley, an unpublished paper given at Temple University in April, 1979, as part of a conference entitled *Illuminating Dance.*
3. Ibid.
4. Joseph Margolis, an unpublished paper delivered at *Illuminating Dance.*
5. For an account of post-modern dance see Sally Banes: *Terpsichore in Sneakers* (Boston: Houghton Mifflin, 1980).

6. Quoted in Bruce Galser: "Questions to Stella and Judd," in *Minimal Art:* ed. G. Battcock (New York: Dutton, 1968), p. 158.

7. Banes discusses the piece on p. 60. The score for the dance is on pp. 71-74.

8. Marcia B. Siegel: *The Shapes of Change* (Boston: Houghton Mifflin, 1980), pp. 73-74.

9. Rainer's extremely lucid and compelling explication of *Trio A,* which my account follows in many respects, can be found in *Minimal Art,* pp. 263-273. It is entitled "A Quasi Survey of Some 'Minimalist' Tendencies in the Quantitatively Minimal Dance Activity midst the Plethora, or an Analysis of *Trio A.*"

DISCUSSION FOLLOWING
NOËL CARROLL PRESENTATION

Panelists: Deborah Jowitt, Senta Driver, Paul Ziff, Noël Carroll, Gerald Myers

DEBORAH JOWITT: I think there are several senses, as Noël has pointed out, in which "expressive" is applied to dance, and I think they're confusing sometimes. There is "expressive" meaning "emotive." The dancer as performer expressing jealousy or rage—feelings. There is the sense in which it is expressive as Monroe Beardsley uses it, I think, a superfluity of expressiveness, meaning I don't just reach my arm, I *reach* my arm—that full-charged, kind of burnished look we recognize as technically-accomplished dancing. I think dance expresses ideas—I really don't know what I think for sure on this, but to me an idea such as Rainer's, a polemical idea about the nature of dance, an anti-dance dance is a material of the dance in the same way Othello's jealousy, the plot part of it, is a material, an element, maybe, in *The Moor's Pavane.* It's the old argument: if it's really ideas you care about expressing, you wouldn't necessarily make a dance to express the ideas. Dance does something the word doesn't do; otherwise the dancers would stay home and make posters. But I think there's another sense of "expressive" I recognize, and it's probably the sense I understand Suzanne Langer to give it, when she says an art is a symbolic form expressive of human feeling. What she means by "feeling," at least as I understand it, is not necessarily love, or hate or fear, but a

104

human response to the forces of the universe as felt—that is, gravity. We all know there is a formula to express gravity mathematically or scientifically, there are other ways of explaining or designating gravity, but dance articulates gravity as felt by us, when we miss a step going down the stairs or when we fall or when we try not to fall or lose equilibrium. Or in Noël's example of Steve Paxton's *Satisfying Lover*, of crowding, of the feeling of crowding, of space shrinking and growing, in that sense any dance to me has to be expressive or not be dance. I do think of Rainer's dance, *Trio A*, as expressive in this particular sense of the word. I can say it does express certain factors about space, tensions in space, weight, time, without in the least disagreeing with Noël's characterization of it as factual or neutral. In fact, even on another level of expressiveness you could perhaps say the dance gives an illusion of inexpressiveness or neutrality as part of the style.

But I do disagree with Noël on one point I've already argued with him. I do think *Trio A* has arresting gestural shapes and if any dancers stay to see the film, I would like to see how many of you could perform how much of it in some semblance of the correct style when it's over, because I've seen the dance once in 1966, once in 1968 and once recently, with no intention of learning the dance. Yet I can tell you the first movement in the dance is this . . . . and this is another (Deborah Jowitt illustrates).

SENTA DRIVER: Let the record show she wraps her arms around her body in a neutral fashion. The leg rises into an arabesque of sorts. The arms revolve in space, and the right leg rises and the weight shifts.

JOWITT: And so I guess I quarrel with what Rainer has said about what she was doing. But I certainly have no quarrel with Noël's characterization of this as factual, or if you want to say "nonexpressive" in the traditional sense either of fully attenuated gesture or of emotional projection by the dancer. I think those are two points, but I think they connect somehow. I'm not sure.

DRIVER: Rainer had said "No" to music, "No" to rules, "No" to virtuosity. It was a very telling statement. I'm wondering if we are simply insisting upon finding this movement expressive, finding it memorable, finding it full of content—in her teeth. If it is possible, I would like to learn to look at something so I do not force expressiveness or content into it. I would like to go as far as I can in following her down that road, and that has a lot to do with training your eye and considering her arguments and stripping away. Perhaps there is more we have to strip away from our perception of it. I'm sure she wouldn't object greatly to your making something of this piece. We're always groping for what to say about a work when we see it. What does it mean? Is it now discredited? People generally know they are not supposed to ask that question because choreographers will frown and snarl. But people wonder, "What does it add up to? Does it amount to anything? Does it make its point?" We're all backing around the same question. Is this a pointless and useless work, or is this telling in some way? I'm not suggesting we should walk away from *Trio A* and have no reaction and erase it as it happens. But is there some other way to look?

Memory is different from interpretation. There is a movement you forgot in it, Debbie; there is something about pulling the elbow back. I remember its energy. I can't remember how many times I have seen it. I once saw it performed backwards by an enterprising young choreographer, I'm sure with Rainer's blessing, and I have a very strong impression of this remarkable flow of neutral energy. It's not airless. It is alive. It is monotonic, but if you've ever attempted to use a monotone rigorously it's almost impossible to say a monotone, and it's probably almost impossible to perform a monotone. Another confusing element here is the quality of the performer. Whether they are trained or not, some people have such resonance and such energy and such *je ne sais quoi* that they become expressive media through which *Trio A* is distorted or revealed or tempered in some way. And you aren't going to see *Trio A* without a performer. I'm sure Rainer would like to stage *Trio A* with no performer, but she hasn't managed to do that yet. That may be one reason why we jump to a conclusion that there is something going on here.

I think there is a difference between a proposition or a demonstration and an act of expression. I think of it as a two-part thing or a one-part thing. I don't think you can look at most of this kind of work, not just *Trio A* but so many people's work now, and try to find a separate piece of baggage that is its meaning or its import or its thrust or point, or whatever, because often the pieces are themselves their own message. They are sometimes their own commentary. They are sometimes the snake with its tail in its mouth. They consume themselves. I can't tell you yet whether that's an expressive act: it's a remarkable fact. I need a couple of days to consider this question. I will yield to Mr. Ziff.

PAUL ZIFF: Well, I take it the avowed aim of this dance is to express nothing: it's supposed to express nothing. And Noël has said it expresses something. I don't see any difficulty at all. It would be an elementary confusion to think there is a contradiction here. I think the dance may very well express nothing and in so doing could be said to express something. Now I may sound like I'm talking in a very funny way, but there are lots of analogies here. Think of a legalistic distinction between acts of omission and genuine acts where you actively do something. If I perform an act of omission, then in a very straightforward sense I've done something and I may even be legally responsible for it. Yet, in a very good sense I could say, "I did nothing," and the charge is that doing nothing in that case was doing something.

Now, the thing I liked about Noël's account was that he made clear the sense in which expressing nothing was to express something, and that it's inevitable in the context of the dance. Because, given that you view this as a dance in its historical setting, and given that the dance is designed to reject everything you can think of in connection with the dance, in so doing it's expressing all that. It also is expressing nothing in the explicit sense in which the choreographer intended. So I don't really see any great problem here. This is sort of the limiting case of expression, but it's a fact that if you embed the dance in the context of a performance and display it, then there is no way you can avoid to so take it. If the choreographer really wished to achieve the aim of not only expressing nothing but also in doing that expressing nothing, then the thing to do would be not to show the film. I mean I have heard of artists who did a painting and immediately burnt it, in which case that painting expressed nothing. It was meant to express nothing and it did indeed express nothing. I suppose it was an act of futility on the part of the artist. I don't know what satisfaction he got out of it, but short of that, the dance will express something, but nonetheless may express nothing in a very interesting way.

NOËL CARROLL: I was very interested in a point Senta made

relevant to something I think the dance is saying. Senta expressed a desire to see movement bereft of the expressive qualities, to see in a counter-conventional way, and I think sentiment is something that animated the creation of *Trio A*. I want, though, to point out this is a very special kind of desire to have. It's a desire I think could probably be more specifically located, but I like alliteration, so I'll call it a "post-positivist" desire. I think the way in which this dance is factual has connotations of "factuality" that are particularly modern notions of factuality.

Why do I bring that up? Well, I want to tie into some things we ended on last night. This may be a way of doing it. Last night, when we were talking, there were a couple of unresolved strands in the conversation. Two are particularly interesting. One is Debbie's worry about our submerging the dance in words, and other is Paul Ziff's response to my point about the importance of homologies in figuring our expressions. How do we ground those homologies if not in physiognomic qualities? Well, what I think is especially interesting about Senta's remark is that these expressive qualities, what I was calling anthropomorphic qualities, things like factuality, to a certain extent do pick up their connotations in language. The interplay between theory, language, dance, and in fact all the other arts, is very intense and is a source of creativity. Senta pointed out many people have read Rainer and seen Rainer and then been emboldened to strike out on new paths. And they do that, I think, because of the inter-animation of language and dance and the inter-animation of all aspects of culture. It is important to see all of this material as inter-animating and in constant change. Language changes, and theories change, and culture changes the meanings of movements and change the possible meanings of movement. There couldn't have been, I want to argue, a "factual" dance in the Middle Ages. And partially in answer to Paul Ziff, I want to say one reason I'm not convinced physiognomic qualities will do all of our theoretical work for us is that there are some anthropomorphic qualities like factuality. They would be very hard to think of as physiognomically grounded, because a strong part of their connotations grows with history. There couldn't be the possibility of attributing factuality as an expressive quality, I think, to a building or to a painting or to a movement until after the nineteenth century.

ZIFF: Could I just object to one thing. I didn't suppose all qualities would be grounded in physiognomic characteristics. Obviously, if you told a narrative or had it associated with the dance, then the language is going to get into the act right away, and to suppose physiognomic characteristics explained everything in the dance would be to suppose it explained everything in language, and that would simply be idiotic.

CARROLL: I'm sorry if I accused you of that.

GERALD MYERS: I think the audience might appreciate hearing from one of the choreographers working in New York who is sympathetic to seeing something called in the broad sense "non-expressive" dance. What is it, Senta, that appeals to you in this?

DRIVER: In the possibility of non-expressive dance?

MYERS: Yes.

DRIVER: I don't use this term of my work, partly because I hadn't thought in those terms. I certainly have been interested in notions. I think of myself as conceptually governed. I am usually trying to demonstrate notions. I think of that as a factual or information-giving thing. I'm interested in teasing out movement to show things, to perhaps prove things, to draw distinctions between things. Some of my works turn out not to be dances but to be articles. I'm still in an early stage. I have been described as didactic, which always strikes me as teaching run amuck. That's probably not inaccurate in some way. I'm interested in all the new possibilities of seeing and of learning things.

We can talk about a work in which there was no movement. We can tell you why we thought it was a dance. There has been one very noteworthy work that Debbie and I have discussed, and that has been very influential, in which the dancer appeared in a completely still form for four hours a day for a month or more, and I still think of that as an act of movement, partly because the performer was not dead. That actually was a very emotionally-resonant situation. I don't know what the choreographer, Douglas Dunn, would think. I would argue with him that his work was expressive in the usual sense, in the Limón sense. It conveyed a situation. It caused strong emotional reactions in people, some of which they then attached to the performer, which is our fallacy but it does happen. If you move me, I think you are moving. If you terrify me, I think you are frightening, and I think you were trying to be, in a performance situation.

Every time I see a contradiction or hear about something that can't be done or something that goes against all received notions, I immediately want either to see an example of it or try to make an example of it. In that sense, the history of dance since Judson in 1961 has been perverse. But it has yielded extraordinary new things. The interesting thing to me is that, since Rainer, uninflected gesture, long portions of movement without climax and without rhythmic accent of the usual sort, have become very popular. Many people have used it and our eye has simply adjusted so that we now see flows of energy and microscopic stops and starts that we find rhythmic, whether they were intended or not. That's a question of the eye growing used to what it could not formerly see.

MYERS: Deborah, I'd like to ask whether these dances succeed in being expressive or not in Noël's terms. What do you think is going on right now in the environment, in the culture, that makes dancers reach for a non-expressive medium?

JOWITT: I don't think they are doing that anymore, certainly not to the degree that they were when Rainer made *Trio A*. I think, like any art, dance tends to go in cycles, and the Judson movement of the Sixties, as I see it, was, in part, a reaction to the art of the preceding generation. Perhaps not Graham herself or Limón himself, but many of the new generation felt that dance, modern dance particularly, had become ornate, preoccupied with glamor, drama, virtuosity, and had lost some of its original purity of purpose without finding any new purpose, and was simply feeding off itself. That's not uncommon in art, and I think their reaction was very strong and was a kind of Cartesian process of stripping away everything. And that's what I think of Rainer's 1965 statement that said, "No" to spectacle, "No" to virtuosity, "No" to moving and being moved— all those things which she later retracted bit by bit, when she came to understand the level on which she could deal with them. But in those days she was saying, "If I take away everything, everything, what am I left with? What is the most basic factor that I can still call a dance?" In that period we had people who took baths on stage and called them dances. Or like Steve Paxton's *Intravenous Lecture* which was a protest dance about not being able to perform *Satisfying Lover* with forty-two naked redheaded people, because of censorship, and so he walked around with a bottle and something dripping into his vein and seemed to be saying in part, "Is this more obscene or any more difficult for you to look at than forty-two naked red-headed people?" There were a lot of polemic dances about clearing the air. Rainer herself said, much later, words to this effect: "Many in the dance community are still preoccupied with basic uses of weight, space, shape, time. Most of it is a dead bore." And she is now in film, but just before she went into film she was beginning to use fiction and biography as a material ingredient in dance with the same factual, clinical method she had used before.

So it was a reaction against an existing art and also perhaps a comment on the times. Modern dance had become super-charged and the Judson people wanted to express a different kind of rhythm. It was their way of following some of the tenets of John Cage, which had to do, not with making art more accessible to the common man, but with making it more like the processes of daily life and therefore less hermetic. I think Rainer did what she did in those days because she wanted to force us to look at movement for what it was rather than with some preconception of what it meant or some slant from her as to what it ought to mean. That's all. I saw Deborah Hay's dance that Michael Kirby wrote an entire chapter about in his wonderful book, *The Art of Time*, and which he called "objective dance" because it was object-like: it was objective in the sense that it induced no kinaesthetic response in the spectator. But although my kinetic response was minimal and not very pleasant, perhaps, it was there.

CARROLL: I also think you would simply describe it as an attempt to articulate in dance things that were vitally of interest in different parts of the culture, especially in the Sixties the influence of painting and sculpture and the rhetoric of painting and sculpture. There are interesting interrelationships between those, too. Judson Church and the experimentation influenced dance critics, or at least some dance critics, who became far more interested than previous dance critics in a kind of descriptive criticism, a kind of seeing of the dance as movement, and brought in a more rigorous sort of criticism, a moving away from previous impressionistic criticism to a more scientific level: in some cases, a phenomenological mode of description, and in other cases an interest in the different kinds of notation systems. There was a terrific amount of cross-fertilization in the direction of heightened rigor which, metaphorically, you might describe as a kind of Cartesianism, only in the sense of attempts to get to the bottom of things.

MYERS: Sometimes you get very interesting answers if you throw questions to someone who thinks he doesn't have anything really very special to say on the matter. I asked Paul in a telephone conversation, "Why do you think dance is so popular today in our culture?" And he said, "Well, everything is popular. There's just more people." Paul, do you think a dance which seeks to be expressive of something by virtue of expressing nothing is going to be very popular in our culture? What's its future?

ZIFF: I don't know. I've not really thought about that. I rather doubt it, because I think to express nothing in dance would call for such extreme control. I mean, obviously, you are going to have to limit the character of the movements. This really ties into a difficult question I've been sitting here thinking about. If you view dance, as I want to, as a symbolic system, the dance that isn't expressive would be a dance that had a very clear syntactic structure but had no semantic values assigned to it, and that raises the question of how the semantic values are assigned. Now, if they are assigned naturally, if we just have a tendency to interpret movements in a certain way, if they have this emotional quality built into the movement, then to produce a non-expressive dance will call for enormous control. I don't mean necessarily control on the part of the dancer, but control on the part of the choreographer. And there will be a very severe limitation on what can be done. Now, that's not going to be vastly popular.

Nothing in art that makes great demands is ever terribly popular. The thing about popular art is that it makes minimal demands on the performers very often, and generally on the audience. Disco dancing, which is the rage right now, is terribly popular, but it is remarkably expressive. I don't particularly like what it expresses. Every time I see disco dancing I get very turned off. That's just a peculiarity of mine. But if anyone would say that's not expressive, I think they would be mad. It shows all kinds of rather extraordinary sentiments, feelings and the like. I don't see how people who do it could possibly refrain from expressing what they are expressing. And so I can't imagine non-expressive art would ever grab the public any more than the attempt to write boring books would create a best seller. I mean, somebody may achieve a boring novel by intent but it would be a miracle if it became a best seller. I'll give you one very good example: *Finnegan's Wake* is a carefully-designed work which makes maximal demands on the reader and is as carefully contrived as you can imagine anything is, but no one can read it. I mean, no one really reads it. I think William Empson gave a good description of it: "*Finnegan's Wake* is a corpse." And I think the opposite end of the spectrum would be exactly the same. The infinitely boring book would be a nice example to have on your bookshelf, but you're not going to read it.

DRIVER: I think we're getting a little confused here. I don't think Rainer intended to be boring or repulsive. I think she wanted to know if there was enough there if you stripped away the extra baggage. I think she wanted to consist. She wanted to present. The work exists. There was no question here of destroying the dance. I think we have had people who have made dances that cannot be perceived at all. They can only be considered. People in the correspondence school of thought. This work exists and is, I think, very influential. It may not reach a wide audience, but it can triumph equally by infecting everything, or a great deal of what comes after it. But it does have a persistence. It has a very strong existence. We are still arguing about it. To write a boring novel is to attempt to influence the audience in a very specific way, which is emotional after all. That's an expressive aim.

MYERS: Are there questions in the audience?

AUDIENCE: I'm interested in taking up Debbie's comments about the feeling that's expressed in human movement. I'm wondering if the Laban-notated score of *The Moor's Pavane* is expressive, as the dance is expressive when it's performed? Why didn't Yvonne Rainer choose to make moving sculpture? Would she, if she had the choice available to her, have her dance performed by programmed robots?

JOWITT: I think a Labanotation score has the same relationship to *The Moor's Pavane* as, to use Mr. Ziff's example, a road map may have to a route. It is another kind of symbolic system and it is denotative of that movement. It's not expressive in that sense. About robots: not only was she not interested in having her dance performed by robots, but midway in the long career of *Trio A* there was a performance in which a group of students who had just learned it performed it in public, in silence, and then she sent out the militia—Steve Paxton, David Gordon, the Judson group, who did it, as I remember to a Rolling Stones record. And all those inexpressive, non-expressive, completely casual dancers, with this background music, suddenly looked like the most ravishing, charismatic performers you could imagine, because by then she had begun to investigate the differences performance made on the material, and that was very important to her, and I think she was generous with the material itself. Everybody who learned *Trio A* one summer in 1969 at Connecticut had the right to reproduce it, teach it, give it. She gave it as a gift. Although she said recently she finally met a *Trio A* she didn't like.

Is Dance Elitist?

Presented by
Thomas E. Wartenberg

THE QUESTION UPON WHICH I would like to focus
our attention tonight is whether dance is necessarily an elitist art
form. This question achieves a particular degree of urgency when
one considers the nature of the institutional setting within which the
dialogue we are conducting tonight is taking place. Here we sit, on
the lawn of Duke University, a group of individuals dedicated in one
way or another to dance as an art form. We are here because of our
learning, our skill, some virtue or other, depending on who we are.
Some of us have these characteristics only potentially, not yet having made it on our own, but that is secondary. The crucial point is
that the New York style of elegance we see and hear is quite foreign
to the culture that exists at the fringes of this campus.

This juxtaposition became more unsettling to me (I had not intended to talk about it specifically) because of the performance that

composed the gala opening of the Festival this year. What we were treated to was the spectacle of North Carolinians, many from the Durham area, people for whom dance is a form of recreation and, we might expect, expression, performing their homespun dances for us on the stage of Page Auditorium. And the "us" included the President of Duke University and a representative of the Governor of North Carolina. And at the same time we heard these people praising the Festival for bringing dance to North Carolina, we were exposed to a group of ordinary folk doing for us what they do for themselves—that is, dance.

And I have to admit I felt pretty angry at that performance. For I felt a good deal of condescension in the choices that led to it and in the attitudes of those that watched it. And so I decided I wanted to force the issue, to raise it here in this forum tonight, to get us to confront the question of what we find valuable in dance and whether that valuable quality doesn't force an elitism upon us.

Dance is, of course, a varied cultural form. From the rather simple steps of the clogger to the spectacular leaps of Mikhail Baryshnikov, from the form of a religious ritual to a gala event costing $100 a seat on Broadway, dance still exists in many forms and is performed in many different ways. My concern tonight, however, is with modern dance, that form of dance which is the primary interest of most of us here. And the question I want to pose for our mutual consideration is whether the form modern dance has taken in our culture causes it to be an elitist art form.

To begin with, it is important that we understand what we mean by "elitism." Especially with a word like this, whose associations are so emotionally colored, it is important to specify what we are going to mean by it. While I realize using that term may well produce reactions that get in the way of conducting the rational discourse I take to be the purpose of philosophy and of our discussion here tonight, I am not using that term as part of a polemical argument, as a way of branding my opponents. And I hope we all can follow suit in trying to move beyond a pure emotional response to that word. I am using it because it conveys a certain idea, an idea whose precise meaning I will now try to specify.

What I mean by "elitism" is the assumption that human beings can be divided into two (or more) groups, one of which is necessarily superior to the other(s), as the result of possessing a certain characteristic. Any sort of aristocratic society, for example, is elitist when it makes a distinction between the members of the society based on blood relations. To say an art form is elitist is to say it underscores such a hierarchy of human beings by its presentation of human life. Much of Western religious art is hierarchical, to choose an example to illustrate this point. If we have a picture of the cruficixion, and the multitude is grouped about Jesus in an order that follows an established hierarchy, we have an example of elitism in painting.

The alternative to elitism is an egalitarian or democratic spirit, which attributes to each human being a fundamental dignity, viewing all distinctions between persons as secondary to their fundamental equality. Rather than accepting any fundamental division of humanity into groups of differing desert, democratically inspired art sees all human beings as equally worthy. A good deal of late nineteenth-century art is democratic in this sense, for it tries to show common people as fitting subjects for treatment in what had been an aristocratic medium and as therefore worthy of our aesthetic concern.

It is important to realize this definition of elitist versus democratic art does not square with the more traditional dichotomies of folk versus skilled art or high versus low culture. What differentiates the two types of art I am talking about is not the amount of skill or expertise necessary to produce or understand it, but rather the assumptions about human beings that underline it. A piece of folk art can be expressive of a belief in a hierarchical culture, just as a work of high culture can be profoundly democratic. The grounds of my distinction is the content or significance of the work and its system of signification, rather than a social or aesthetic element.

Again, many people take "elitism" to refer to the sort of audience a piece is directed toward. This is not the use of the word I intend. A work does not have to be intended for a mass audience to be democratic in the sense I shall use the word.

What I am trying to isolate is a fundamental dichotomy in the nature of art. I want to be able to speak of democratic, non-elitist art in the sense of an art which confirms the greatness of the human spirit in the face of all attempts to demean that spirit, to make people accept a diminished sense of their own worth, by the use of hierarchical dichotomies. As we shall see, such art is not necessarily an art for immediate consumption. Rather, it is an art designed to further the cause of human emancipation.

In this regard, it stands opposed to what I have called elitist art, an art that affirms ultimate distinctions between people. Surprisingly, I think a good deal of mass culture is elitist in this sense, for it operates in an acceptance of social, economic and political differences that confine rather than expand the human spirit.

The examples I have given so far of the distinction between democratic and elitist art are pretty straightforward. Paintings have contents or meanings and we can distinguish those whose contents are dependent on hierarchical notions and those that are not. The same would hold of theatrical works of art, poems, even novels. However, when we come to dance, we find ourselves in a bind, for there seems no way to extend these distinctions to dance as a whole. While it is true that some dances have meaning in the sense that they employ dramatic situations, many dances do not employ such narrative technique. And even more important, it seems such narrative elements do not form the crucial vehicle by means of which dance communicates. It therefore might seem that we shall be forced to abandon our search for a way of distinguishing between democratic and elitist dance because we are unable to attribute a general meaning to dance.

It is my contention that we do not have to despair of making such a distinction. What we do need to do is to specify the particular means whereby dances do articulate a meaning. Once we have done this, I shall argue, there will be a straightforward way to distinguish elitist from democratic dance.

One thing upon which critics and dancers seem to agree is that dance, while it does manage to communicate with its audience, does so in a non-linguistic or non-discursive manner. It is the sense of movement, rather than words, that is the primary mode of dance signification. Like music and abstract art, dance employs as elements of its "language" items that in themselves are not usually thought of as having meaning. A movement of the arm is no more tied to a specific meaning than a C-sharp or the color yellow, although all of these can acquire a type of meaning in a specific context such as that provided by works of art.

But I want to emphasize my point is not that dance is a language or system of symbolic representation that is analogous to a language and that such a "language" has a cognitive content that is the meaning of dance. Such a view would be true of only dance drama and not the more abstract forms of dance. Instead, I wish to claim that dance selects a certain range of motions as its basic vocabulary of movement and that this very selection process is the basis of dance's conveyal of meaning. For by its selection, dance presents us with an idealized version of human movement. We see, in dance, a human body or human bodies moving in certain specific ways. These manners of movement are ideal in that they are an abstraction from real life motion, an adaptation of recognizable motion to the specified syntax of a dance. But they are also ideal in the sense that they are held up as ideals, that is, they present us with a version of the human being as a moving, active creature that is to serve as a grounds for our evaluation of human life.

It is this latter feature of dance, its presentation of an ideal of human life by means of a special syntax of movement, that I see as the central means whereby dance conveys meaning. By giving us a view of certain idealized human motions as fit subjects for our aesthetic approval, dance embodies a set of valuations, a whole sense of the human body and appropriate modes of movement and conduct. And it is this sense of the nature of the human being that can be elitist or democratic. A dance form will be elitist if the style of movement it uses as its syntax is clearly identifiable as fitting the style of movement of a certain class. Democratic dance, on the contrary, will be supportive of each individual human being's sense of himself or herself and not set up any fundamental dichotomy of human worth.

Now it certainly is true that dance, as a performing art, has an elitist heritage in this sense. And I don't simply mean by this that ballet, which was, as John Martin points out, the first secular dance,[1] originated in the aristocratic courts of Europe out of social dance forms. Rather, I mean the style of movement held out by ballet as an ideal for men and women is one that has an essentially elitist or hierarchical bias.

In order to see this, listen to the following definition of dance, proposed by John Weaver, in 1721:

> Dance is an elegant, and regular movement, harmoniously composed of beautiful attitudes, and contrasted graceful postures of the body, and parts thereof.[2]

What Weaver sees as the essence of dance is a certain elegance, a refined sense of movement, much in keeping with the aristocratic courts of his time. I want to suggest that, at base, such a view of the essence of dance serves an elitist function in that it causes us to look at normal movement in terms of the aesthetic distinctions it sets up. Only those capable of such graceful postures are deemed acceptable, beautiful. And therefore the social divisions at the root of such grace or lack of it are underscored by such valuations.

We can see how such a definition of dance can come to serve as the basis of an evaluation of people in terms of the aesthetic canons of taste it articulates in some remarks made by Gaston Vuillier in 1897:

> Like poetry and music, to which it is closely allied . . . the choreographic art . . . was probably unknown to the earlier ages of humanity. Savage man, wandering in forests, devouring the quivering flesh of his spoils, can have known nothing of those rhythmic postures which reflect sweet and caressing sensations entirely alien to his moods. The nearest approach to such must have been the leaps and bounds, the incoherent gestures, by which he experienced the joys and furies of his brutal life.[3]

Vuillier begins by articulating a triumvirate of arts—poetry, music, choreography—and, except for a feeling of discomfort with his focus on the design rather than the product, this seems fine to us. We can even manage to agree with the claim that such "arts" as choreography did not exist in earlier epochs, if for no other reason than that the division of labor necessary to support them as occupations had not arisen. But when we come to the idea of "savage man . . . devouring the quivering flesh of his spoils" as opposed to "the rhythmic postures which reflect sweet and caressing sensations," we sense with discomfort a sensibility far from our own. The rigid dichotomy between savage and civilized people is something we do not accept. The condescension embodied in the notion of the emotional lives of such "brutes" is so striking, I hardly need dwell upon it.

But what I do want to stress, at the risk of being a little overbearing, is that the elitism, the condescension, the hierarchical sense of things implicit in Vuillier's remarks has a real, concrete basis in the aesthetic canons of nineteenth-century ballet and the sense of graceful movement it applauds. When we think about ballet, we think of rigidly-held bodies and delicately-structured movements, the sorts of conventions of motion that contribute to the ethereal nature of the impression made by the ballet. We see men and women inhabiting a world, but it is a world with no loose edges, no wasted motions. It is the aristocratic dream: a world of pure form, drained of any raucous emotions in its inhabitants and shielded from any untoward influence by others not suited to such an ethereal realm.

What I'm claiming is that ballet of this type, by its very vocabulary of movement, instantiates a hierarchical, elitist view of human beings. For the movements it presents for our inspection and approval validate (or demean) certain images of maleness, of femaleness, of humanity. And they set up a dichotomy between gracefulness and awkwardness that is, at root, elitist.

The flip side of the refinement of the sensibility to which the ballet appeals is a blindness to the validity, the expressiveness of all forms of movement other than those admitted by the official canons of taste. Behind the use of terms like "savage" by Vuillier is a failure to recognize forms of movement alternative to those sanctioned by the courts of nineteenth-century Europe as fit subjects for aesthetic approval. Rather than seeing, behind those distinct forms of movement ritualized by different cultures, a common attempt to use movement as a means of expression and communication, the elitist temper of the ballet sets itself apart as a unique form of human experience, human culture, artistic creativeness.

If all this demonstrates that the balletic tradition has an elitist component, this elitist heritage is something dance shares with many other art forms—music, for instance. And yet it is just as crucial to note dance also has its roots in human cultural traditions that are anything but elite. In many ways, dance has a better claim to being originally a democratic form, for dance was a part of early religious rituals during which the human spirit was celebrated. Such ritualistic use of dance can be seen as democratic insofar as it celebrated the underlying value of human life regardless of social distinctions. The celebration of the human body as a vehicle of spiritual activity entails a democratic stance, a validation of the human in any form in which it appears.

This attitude is also embodied in traditional folk dance, a cultural form in which dance is a mode of participation rather than performance. The great folk ritual, in which all meet as equals in a democratic celebration of life itself, is a primary democratic social form.

One way to think about the mission the originators of modern dance took upon themselves is that they tried to shape the spirit behind such democratic forms of dance into a manner of artistic performance suitable to the cultural traditions of the twentieth century. Isadora Duncan's oft-quoted vision can serve as a sort of emblem of this view. She tells us of her vision in the following words:

> great strides, leaps and bounds, lifted foreheads and farflung arms, dancing the language of our pioneers, the fortitude of our heroes, the justice, kindness, purity of our women and, through it all the inspired love and tenderness of our mothers, that will be American dancing.[4]

What we have here is a vision of dance that is a far cry from the rigidities of traditional ballet. Aside from the democratic spirit that sees dance as the province of all Americans and not just of a single class, Isadora's stress on bold expressive movements shows a further attempt to democratize the very language of dance. Dance is to become expressive of a deep-felt democratic spirit, it is to depict that spirit in its performance and it is to become the visible spirit of an entire nation. All of these are different senses in which Isadora's vision is of a democratic dance.

But the one idea I want to emphasize is Isadora's appeal to specific bodily movements that are a departure from the placid movements of nineteenth-century ballet. What Isadora saw in these movements, movements more akin to those Vuillier attributes to savages than to civilized people, movements Isadora was able to read into the gestures frozen on Greek urns, was a democratic language of dance, a language able to express what she saw as the American tradition in the dance medium. The point of her remarks is not that we ought to dance pioneer stories, but that the incorporation of a non-balletic vocabulary into dance would enable dance to be democratic in the way Isadora saw the pioneers as being, to allow each individual a means of expressing himself or herself with dance movement.

This vision of a new, democratic dance was common to many of the founders of modern dance. Doris Humphrey, who many see as a key figure in actually realizing a form of dance Isadora was only able to articulate as a vision, puts it this way. Talking of the founders of modern dance, she says:

> The contention of these few is that dance, and dance drama, persistently robust after thousands of years of snubbing by asceticism, scholasticism, and puritanism, can make profound revelations of that which is significant in the relations of human beings, can restore the dignity of the body, which prurience and hypocrisy have damaged, can recall the lost joys of people moving together rhythmically for high purposes, can improve

the education of the young, can, to a much larger extent than it does, restore vitality to the theater, can contribute a moral stimulus to the furtherance of more courageous, coordinated, and cultured behavior.[5]

By revitalizing dance, Humphrey sees the possibility of fighting against the repression inherent in a culture she characterizes as hypocritical. By restoring our bodies to us, modern dance can serve a democratic end.

Whereas nineteenth-century ballet drew a rigid line between its own beautiful forms and the crude "leaps and bounds" of savage peoples, modern dance has been very open to forms of movement used in other cultures. In fact, a number of modern choreographers have seized upon such forms as a valid alternative to the balletic form, for they have seen in such forms an authenticity they have not found in the ballet. What is recognized in such forms is the universality of certain attempts at artistic expression. And it is this that is valued and incorporated in the new forms of movements employed in modern dance.

This very freedom of movement which lies at the basis of modern dance is a prime indication of its democratic nature. By trying to articulate a new sense of the body and its relation to our emotional lives via a new attitude towards movement, modern dance contains a valuation that is at distinct odds with that contained in the traditional ballet. Alwin Nikolais characterizes it as follows:

> Each new perspective of art breaks down another barrier in man's (sic) quest for freedom. The major characteristic of the contemporary vista of dance is freedom. But it is freedom in bondage to the subterranean and primordial poetry of life which permeates all and everything—that which we call Art.[6]

In these words, we hear the hope that dance can be an agent of democracy, a means of giving people a greater degree of control over the shape of their lives, a deeper sense of their own dignity as human beings. This would lend support to my contention that modern dance was conceived of as an avowedly anti-elitist art form, an art form dedicated to the development, in movement, of a democratic vision of the human spirit.

By discarding the traditional, aristocratic vocabulary of nineteenth-century ballet, modern dance embodies in its new vocabulary of movement a fundamentally different set of assumptions about human beings and their lives. No longer is a fixed set of movements set up as definitive of the genre, a set of movements that idealizes, in both the senses I have talked of, aristocratic movement. Although individual choreographers may and do still choose a limited vocabulary for their dance, the dropping of the aristocratic sense of movement opens up the possibility for modern dance to achieve a democratic spirit. This is because there is no longer a single set of movements regarded as the province of beauty, a set of movements derived from the attitudes of a particular class and reflecting their sense of decorum and appropriate behavior. By enlarging the syntax of dance and overthrowing the dominance of a single paradigm of beauty, modern dance entails a reversal of the traditional aesthetic, a reversal that allows us to look at all movement as an appropriate object for aesthetic appraisal. This is an inherently democratic approach in that it breaks apart the hierarchical stance of ballet and opens up to us, by means of its use of movements appropriate to them, all aspects of life as equally valid subjects for approval. No longer is a special set of movements definitive of grace, nor a certain set of emotions or situations identical with life itself. Although dance still proceeds by means of an idealization of life in the movements it uses, the ideal of modern dance is a democratic ideal, not an aristocratic one.

It is important to realize this democratization of dance via an expanded vocabulary of movement does not entail that every choreographer need accept possible movement as part of his or her syntax. Rather, the important feature of this "revolution" is that the dominance of the entire genre by a single set of movements is undercut and thereby the embodiment of an alternative set of assumptions about the nature of human beings is brought into being in dance. And it is this openness, this sense of alternative vocabularies and differing perspectives, that is the kernel of the democratic spirit of modern dance, for it validates each individual's attempt to define for him- or herself an authentic sense of movement, a fitting model for a truly democratic sense of life itself. No longer need we see beautiful movement as the province of a single class. Any movement may be beautiful, depending on how it fits into a choreographer's vision.

Again, let me stress the fact that I see, in this change of dance syntax, a fundamental reversal in the meaning of dance as an art form. From a hierarchical form, intent to encapsulate a slice of aristocratic life, dance has become, at least potentially, a truly democratic art form that presents us with a sense of human life at odds with that of ballet. It is a sense of life supportive of individual human beings and not of a single class.

This sense of dance as a democratic form that I have just outlined is something I have attributed to the art form as a whole. Individual choreographers have a further option of creating a more specific democratic dance by incorporating in their specific syntaxes of movement more democratic forms. If you remember that sexism and racism are both forms of elitism as I have defined it, it will be evident how a dancer's choice of a particular vocabulary can embody a more specific democratic vision. For example, by not allowing the men in a company to support the women in traditional ballet postures, a choreographer can choose to present for our approval movements that are not in harmony with the sexist role models so prevalent in our society. Or by presenting us with idealizations of movements we tend to think of as awkward for our approval, a choreographer may try to show us that grace and beauty are not the exclusive possessions of a single class. These are just examples of the type of choice of dance movement a choreographer could make in order to democratize his or her language. Modern dance encourages such choices by its approach to movement in general. This particular option of creating a specific vocabulary of democratic dance can exist only within the more general democratic form I have outlined as at the basis of modern dance.

But if modern dance is to be faithful to this democratic vision, to really be a non-elitist art form it might seem that it would have to be capable of immediate communication with its audience. The notion of elitism in regard to content would be extended to the range of appeal of the art form. A democracy of meaning, extended to a democracy of taste. We therefore often hear the claim that modern dance, to be non-elitist, needs to communicate immediately with the audience, without any necessary intervention by a special elite interpreter, namely the critic.

While it certainly is true that words are no substitute for dance itself, I want to argue that the attempt to devalue the critical response to dance as elitist and essentially nondemocratic is a mistake. While criticism is not meant to replace dance, it has a necessary function in bringing people to a place where they can respond to dance more fully. For a dance, like any work of art, is a carefully-structured artifact. And, as such, appreciation of that structure may require effort, an effort that can be aided by critical mediation.

The idea that art, in order to be democratic, needs to communicate immediately with its audience is fundamentally in error. First of all, the notion of immediacy as it is used here is an ambiguous one. When we call something "immediate," we make necessary reference to a contrasting mediation. It is a relative notion. As used in this context, I gather the idea is to contrast the immediate experience of a democratic work with the mediated experience required by works that demand critical interpretation for their enjoyment. But all art has to be seen as requiring a certain degree of mediation for its effect. Our experience of dance is mediate in that the motions used in a dance are seen in relation to their significance in our more usual experience. To choose one type of example, in order for a movement of the arms to convey grandeur, we need to see that movement as related to our normal gestural movements. This is one sense in which we can say our experience of dance is mediated by certain assumptions. But it also makes sense to think of the dance itself as mediate in that it is the product of a choreographer's reflections of life. Dance, like all art works, is made by a selection from life of certain aspects that are deemed to be significant and are presented to an audience as such. The importance of these facts is that it makes us see that art results in a highly-structured object, an object whose features need not be assimilated at a glance in order for it to be democratic.

Perhaps, what stands as the ground for this negative attitude towards dance that requires verbal explanation is the notion that such verbal response is but a second-class reflection of the real thing. All we need recall, however, is Plato's dismissal of the arts themselves as mere appearances of an appearance in order to realize the dangers inherent in such an attitude. The artist is himself or herself a reflector and the art work, as well as being a specially-constructed object, is a reflection on and of our normal world. And just as the artist, in this case the choreographer, uses dance as a way to embody his or her reactions to the world around him or her, the critic uses language as a way of responding to the dance he or she witnesses. I want to stress the parallels between the artist and the critic in order to make you see that the critic takes a place beside the artist in the attempt to achieve the level of communication necessary for understanding those highly complex objectives we call works of art.

But all this talk of mediation and immediacy, I can imagine

someone thinking, doesn't meet the issue at hand. The question is whether art, in order to be truly democratic, can afford to be so complex, so obscure that it requires the intervention of a specially-trained sensibility to help people understand it. Art, to be democratic, it might be asserted, has to appeal directly to the very people who compose a democracy of taste.

A full answer to this claim would require a long analysis of the place of art in our contemporary culture. But let me try to make a few gestures in the direction of such an answer. First, we need to distinguish the critic from the reviewer. The reviewer is a rehasher. It is part of his or her task to tell the reader what the work is like so the reader will be in good stead at the next cocktail party he attends, so when the subject of Laura Dean's latest creation comes up, the reader is ready to respond with a curt, knowing dismissal, "Oh, Kisselgoff panned it." But, seriously, the reviewer is an information giver, a supplier to us of facts we need to keep up with "the scene" and to use to determine our own patterns of artistic consumption. Using the reviewers' tastes as guides, we can choose how to best apportion our time and money.

The true critic, however, is more than a supplier of information to potential consumers of art. He or she is someone with a special capacity for articulating the nature of his response to works of art. And by using this capacity, he enables us to respond more fully to such works.

The need for such a voice as an aid in comprehending the nature of works of art is based upon the contradictory nature of truly democratic art in our society. On the one hand, art exists within certain genres. The most revolutionary dance is still a dance and has to be perceived within the tradition of dance. And yet a great artist transforms the tradition he has inherited and uses it in a new way, a way never before conceived of, to articulate his democratic vision. It is therefore a surprise, something not easily comprehended.

Meyer Shapiro, in talking about abstract art, gets holds of this paradoxical feature of such works of art. In the modern world, communication itself has become subject to technical powers and thus, according to Shapiro, "helps to build up and to characterize a world of social relationships that is impersonal, calculated and controlled in its elements, aiming always at efficiency." In a world such as this, democratic art must undercut the normal sense of communication.

The experience of the work of art, like the creation of the work of art itself, is a process ultimately opposed to communication as it is understood now.

When the process of communication has itself become monopolized by commercial powers, when selling has come to predominate over telling, the very conventions of communication become a means of domination over human beings, a hierarchical tool of an elitist culture. If art is to remain true to its democratic vision, its goal of helping human beings achieve as high a degree of freedom and dignity as possible, it must undercut the conventions of communication that have become technically dominated. It is this fact that causes art to appear foreign to most people, an obscure object in the world of clear items presented to us for our consumption. Art becomes hard to understand in contrast to the simple act of appropriation required for taking in items in our cultural context. It is as a result of this that art becomes obscure, requires that it be grappled with in order that one comes to see the conventions used for a non-technically-dominated act of communication to succeed.

> Only a mind opened to the qualities of things, with a habit of discrimination, sensitized by experience and responsive to new forms and ideas, will be prepared for the enjoyment of this art.[7]

What Shapiro makes clear is the paradoxical status of what I have called democratic art in modern society. If art is to free us, it needs to undercut the conventions of normal communication. Only in this way will it be able to affirm the human spirit against the dominant forms of our culture. But this entails that such art will be deemed obscure, for by violating the rules of normal communication, it automatically results in a product that cannot be readily assimilated with the wide-eyed unthinking stares of the TV-saturated consumer. Art, to be truly democratic, needs to violate the rules of mass consumption that dominate our society.

There is one further reason that might be put forward as a reason to see dance that requires criticism as elitist and hence undesirable. For dance might be thought to be more ephemeral than the other arts and, hence, the act of criticism to be exercised on an object that cannot be re-perceived. Whereas it might make sense to criticize a poem or a painting, something we can return to in order to achieve a more full experience of the work once we have received critical enlightenment, the same cannot be true of dance. For dances are not possessable objects of consumption. A dance vanishes as it is danced, and it might therefore be thought that a dance must communicate immediately if it is to communicate at all.

There seem to me to be two major problems with such a view. Firstly, it ignores memory. We can all, to a greater or lesser degree, recall dances we have seen and critical response can use these memories as part of its basis. As a result, a critic can help us understand the nature of a particular dance by employing our memories of it. Although such a procedure is not as likely to succeed as one where we can place the object in front of us, it is no less valid. But also we need to acknowledge that criticism of one piece can help us to understand more than just that piece. It can help make us more sensitive to dance as a whole. So, despite the limitations of criticism due to the nature of the dance medium, I see no reason to deny the validity of criticism on such grounds. And as videotape becomes more accessible, the role of the critic may be made even more vital.

I would like to conclude my talk with a question I hope will structure the discussion that follows this paper. I have tried to show that dance can be both elitist and democratic. Depending upon the fundamental conventions it chooses to employ as its own, dance has served both as a vehicle of hierarchical assumptions that limit the degree of respect enjoyed by the great masses of people, as well as a vehicle of freedom, a means of undercutting the culture's elitist presuppositions. I have also tried to show why, even if dance is a democratic art, the function of the critic is far from redundant. Now the question I want to leave you with is, "Where is modern dance today? Has it remained true to its democratic vision or fallen victim to elitist cultural presuppositions?"

This question asks us to consider the place of modern dance in our contemporary culture. And we need to admit such dance has arrived. There is no longer any need for the embattled tone of voice with which Doris Humphrey defended her dance as a serious art form. Dance now has won a central place on our cultural horizon. Posters of Mikhail Baryshnikov rival those of Guillermo Vilas and John Travolta. Modern dance is "in." But what has acceptance done to its vision?

When modern dance first sought to create a public for itself, dancers tried various approaches. Before artists like Martha Graham and Humphrey were able to create an audience for dance on its own terms, with the help, of course, of this very Festival, others tried to tap various popular cultural forms in an attempt to win an audience.

The question is whether contemporary dance has succeeded at the cost of its democratic vision.

As food for thought, let me propose a statement made by Joseph Mazo, one of the most successful writers on dance. In considering various attempts in the Sixties to infuse modern dance with a greater degree of democracy—and that is Mazo's own word—Mazo winds up with the following conclusion:

> The experiment had value, in pointing out that art is integral to, not separate from, human experience, but it also proved that the artist is the member of an elite, whether he, or others not as gifted, likes it or not. Dance which limits its means of expression to the movements of which an untrained body is capable trims the vocabulary to the choreographic equivalent of baby talk.[8]

Mazo points out that a certain technical skill is a prerequisite to modern dance as it now exists, a technical skill taught so well here at the Festival. And Mazo sees the possession of that skill as being the province of a "gifted elite." Now this sense of elitism is not identical with the one I talked about in this paper. But the condescending tone of his remark, with its implicit dismissal of those attempts to achieve a more democratic dance, seems continuous with a tradition of condescension I have seen as prevalent in dance, a tradition modern dance once tried to undercut. What I think we need to do, therefore, is to pause for a moment and ask ourselves, What has happened to Isadora's democratic vision of America dancing?

NOTES

1. John Martin: *An Introduction to the Dance,* New York, 1939, p. 174.
2. Quoted in Richard Krauss: *History of the Dance in Art and Education,* 1969, p. 5.
3. Ibid.
4. Quoted in Krauss, op. cit., p. 144.
5. "Dance Drama" in Walter Sorell: *The Dance has Many Faces,* New York, 1977, p. 26.
6. "Growth of a Theme" in Sorell, op. cit., p. 232.
7. *Modern Art: the 19th and 20th Centuries,* New York, 1978, p. 223.
8. *Prime Movers,* New York, 1977, p. 275.

DISCUSSION FOLLOWING
THOMAS WARTENBERG PRESENTATION

Panelists: Anna Kisselgoff, Marshall Cohen, Gerald Myers, Laura Dean, Thomas Wartenberg

ANNA KISSELGOFF: I thought we were not going to discuss elitism in terms of the taste to which it appeals, or special skills such as a surgeon's. I think you're talking about hierarchical and non-hierarchical assumptions within the art form itself. And I mean, if you're going to choose Isadora Duncan, who takes a slave culture as a model for her inspiration, I really am not clear on what you're talking about. I also don't feel your idea of nineteenth-century ballet squares with my picture of the nineteenth century. If you're just dealing with twenty years within three hundred years, a part of ballet that was directed toward entertaining certain members of a Russian imperial society, okay, but ballet in the eighteenth and the nineteenth centuries was a very middle-class art. I'm sure you've seen the movie *Children of Paradise* and there you have a very good picture of the theaters on the popular boulevards in which ballet existed as a popular art form.

I think Romantic ballet deals with very ordinary human problems: people having to make choices between good and evil, people who are farmers and peasants and are not concerned with saving their crowns. If today you can accept some sort of surrealist image in any kind of work of art, I think you should be able to accept in a nineteenth-century ballet some metaphor for that kind of illusion or working of the subconscious. It's very possible to look at the nineteenth-century ballets as projections of people's subconscious. And I don't see anything hierarchical in that; I just think it's a myth. To revert back to the old idea that ballet is elitist, and I know you did that to provoke us, and that modern art is democratic, is, I think, taking us back thirty years, and it just doesn't square with the facts.

MARSHALL COHEN: I think there's a certain ambiguity lurking in what Tom says. When he talks about elitism he means mainly to talk about a certain quality of movement, not about explicit subject matter or the social classes to which the art actually appeals.

KISSELGOFF: Can I just break in? I do think the movement is a function of the content.

COHEN: I agree. But back to Tom's point. He wanted to define elitism in terms of a certain quality of movement. And I think his idea is that the traditional vocabulary of ballet—its poses, positions and ideals of physical beauty—are simply those of a certain social class, the aristocracy. And he believes that in accepting that class's standards of beauty and grace we're endorsing that class's view of itself and of the world, its "ideology." To begin with, I'm not confident about the facts. I've never seen an aristocrat in third arabesque and I'm not sure different social classes do (or, if they achieved class consciousness, would) have different views about what's graceful. But even if there *is* some important relation between the movements of classical ballet and those of the aristocratic class, what does this show? Perhaps only that aristocrats have the chance to cultivate grace and beauty in a way others don't. The point may be to create a world in which artisans and laborers can achieve and display grace and refinement in a way that is now not possible. What we see in a ballet may in fact be beautiful and graceful and I'm not persuaded that the movements characteristic of hunched-over peasant women or the poses characteristic of bored assembly-line workers, whatever else they may be, are *beautiful.* This is not to say, of course, that they should play no role in art; the beautiful and the graceful have a special role in the art of ballet that they may not have in other arts. One of these other arts may, of course, be modern dance. But is modern dance committed to the view that such movements are graceful and beautiful, and has it, in any case, exploited them?

Here, however, we come to the ambiguity I mentioned in Tom's remarks. At times he appears to think the cure for elitism is to persuade ourselves that the movement characteristic of non-elite social classes is just as graceful and beautiful as that of the aristocracy. But at other times he seems to mean something quite different by a non-elitist, a democratic art. He seems to mean by a democratic art not one that takes the movements of non-elite classes as an ideal, but one which is democratic in the sense that it is prepared to incorporate any movements at all. But this seems a little like saying a style of music that excludes quarter-tones from its scale, or a style of painting that excludes pastels from its palette, is aristocratic. When he's arguing along these lines, I think Tom is very far from the social arguments he mainly seems interested in. Here he seems to be committing himself to the very dubious view that an art which works in a rigorously-structured, limited medium is objectionable. But if this is objectionable, it's surely not objectionable on political grounds. Democracy isn't committed to adequate representation for pastels—or for contractions and releases either. Ballet is, to be sure, anti-democratic in this sense. It works in a delimited medium. But I'm not sure it's any less expressive than modern dance or politically any less democratic. Certainly its achievements are at least as great, even today. One has only to think of George Balanchine to be clear about that.

GERALD MYERS: I'd like to ask Laura Dean whether it ever crosses the mind of dancers and choreographers that they are or are not involved in an elitist art form. Do they ever talk that way?

LAURA DEAN: I don't think we use that word. We're too poor.
But I would like to get at the different levels involved in the use of the word "elitist." When you are looking at anything, you must look at it historically. If you are going to look at, say, elitist movement, you could look at Balinese dance and say that's very elitist because there's so much technique and so much training in it, and because you have to do exactly those movements. And yet all of this is an integral part of that society. Actually you could consider this democratic because it has a great deal to do with that particular reality those people are living with. Now, you could say being a creative artist and making new movements is very democratic because we have a democracy which gives us the freedom in which we are free to make new movements, to make new visions. On the other hand, you could say it's very elitist, because no one is going to understand it at first, because a new language needs to be created and something new needs to be said.

MYERS: Could I ask Anna to consider Tom's question, "Is modern dance elitist?" How is it with modern dance today?

KISSELGOFF: Modern dance has been an elite, the most elite, form of all, simply because, as John Martin said, modern dance is not a system, it is a point of view. Within the point of view everybody has his or her own idiom and his or her personal form of expression. It's interesting to me that modern dance audiences do not cross over. You will not get the Merce Cunningham audience at

133

an Erick Hawkins performance. You could say modern dance idioms, when you place them back to back, might form a range of expression that supposedly is wider than ballet, which is codified. However, each area of modern dance is extremely restrictive. I don't think you'd want to see the full Martha Graham back fall in a Laura Dean piece because it would be a lapse stylistically. Modern dance is not becoming elitist; it always was. It was brought up in the academic institutions of this country. That was the way it could develop. Every college girl took modern dance. And at one time not everybody went to college

The whole thrust of ballet in the Soviet Union, of course, has been to reach the largest audience possible. Therefore you broaden the gesture to make it as communicable as possible to a mass audience. You incorporate acrobatic movement. You reach a dead end, finally, by cutting the dance element out of dance. And you have silent plays. One of the most magnificent productions I've seen from the Soviet Union was a full-evening production of *Othello* in which there was not one dance step. It was all silent acting, and it was terribly faithful to the text, to all the imagery Shakespeare used. However, in its effort to incorporate non-elitist gesture, Soviet ballet finally cut out dance. You had a ballet production with no dance in it.

TOM WARTENBERG: As I previously said, the word "elitism" excites emotions, and I think it has done so here. The word can be used in many different contexts, but what I've tried to do is to isolate one central meaning of the word "elitist" in contrast with democratic, and to talk about that.

KISSELGOFF: Are you dealing only with formal qualities of movement? Is that what you are dealing with?

WARTENBERG: Primarily, yes. I wasn't making the contrast between democratic and elitist on the basis of content. I'm not saying we should see a ballet as democratic if it is a story about peasants.

KISSELGOFF: You don't think the movement is related to the content?

WARTENBERG: In the first place, a lot of dances don't have

meanings in the sense that they tell a story. I was trying to think about the ways in which dance conveys meaning to us. It seems to me one of the primary meanings that's conveyed by dance is a sense of what it is to be a person, the nature of the body, physical movements. The special thrill of watching the dance is to get some sense of the nature of the body, of how the body relates to movement. And it is this sense that is primarily conveyed by dance, and therefore the primary dichotomy in dance between elitism and democratic has to relate to that notion.

COHEN: Classical ballet was directed to the ideal of beauty, and therefore emphasized beautiful movements and beautiful poses. Not all beautiful movements and poses; rather, a limited array of them. And it built on this "vocabulary." So I think what Tom says is *in part* true, but I don't find it objectionable. One of the factors that contributes to the greatness of ballet is its tradition, going back many hundreds of years. The modern ballet choreographer inherits a very refined, subtle medium, one that incorporates the discoveries of many great choreographers. Each modern dancer starts more or less from scratch and there isn't any cumulative elaboration of the medium, any testing of its possibilities. It's not that something wonderful can't be done with it; wonderful things have been done with it. But not as wonderful as the things that have been done in ballet. But that's a bit off the point. The main point is to accept what Tom says, at least to this extent. Traditionally, at least, ballet did put a strong emphasis on cultivating certain special qualities—those of grace, beauty, harmony. It's one of the few arts that still does so and this may be part of the explanation of its current popularity. Certainly it's one reason we love ballet so deeply, one reason to cherish and preserve it. But ballet can display these qualities without committing itself to any particular class's conception of them (if, indeed, these qualities are relativistic in that way). Certainly it needn't, and doesn't, make any such commitment at the present time.

CHARLES REINHART (in audience): You have been speaking of grace, beauty, harmony and two hundred years of tradition. Ballet does have this history behind it. But I want to correct the idea that modern dance is something without roots or lineage. Although modern dance is still in its youth—its "creative" period—there is a family tree and its generations are linked. The great creators who are

135

making our modern dance heritage today learned their rules before they broke them.

WARTENBERG: I would like to reiterate something I said a few moments ago. The word "elitism" seems to have touched off a bit of a powder keg here. When I criticize ballet for having an elitist aesthetics at its base, there are many things I am not claiming. I am not saying dance needs to appeal to all people at all times and any dance that doesn't do this is non-democratic. Laura and Anna are right to say modern dance is elitist insofar as its audience appeal is concerned. But that is not what I am talking about. Nor am I saying just because the dancers in a ballet happen to be peasants, the ballet will be democratic. That is to accept an analysis of elitism based upon the content of a dance. As I have tried to stress, the notion of elitism I have been working with is based on the style of movement, the aesthetic ideals, to borrow a term from Marshall's paper, that a given type of dance incorporates. And what I have been trying to point out is that modern dance, in contradistinction to ballet, has a democratic vocabulary of movement.

Now, Marshall points out that there can be some misunderstanding of what I am saying. One might be inclined to say that so long as a form of art incorporates *any* special set of movements it is elitist, that to be truly democratic a dance form would have to allow any movement whatsoever into its vocabulary. I think such a view is certainly wrong. We won't get interesting dances without some sort of technique being used in the dancing. Even folk dances have a specific set of steps that can be performed with varying degrees of success and style. To outlaw all technique, to argue for the inclusion of every movement, with no regard for quality, is indeed to push a view that threatens the existence of art itself. And that is not what I have been doing here today.

What I have been trying to claim is that the specific ideals of motion incorporated in classical ballet are elitist in that they posit as ideal a set of characteristics of motion that are part of the sense of refinement one associates with the upper classes of society. By only allowing these movements that are "graceful" in the sense of appearing graceful to members of the court to count as fit for our viewing in a dance, we implicitly endorse the very valuation of movement which says only aristocrats can be graceful. Marshall seems to be comfortable with that. I am not. I think there is as much grace in the actions of ordinary human beings as there is in the movements of the court nobility. Whether that is true or not is something we can discuss. But the crucial point I am trying to make is that the notion of elitism I am using in my presentation is different from one that is being discussed here. It is a sense of elitism based on the quality of movement in the sense I have just tried to indicate and not some of the other senses that are being attributed to me.

Let me end with a brief comment on Isadora. Isadora got her inspiration for dance from looking at Greek urns, not from studying the movement of Greek aristocrats. So I don't think you can use her as a counter-example to my claim. What she saw in Greek urns was, I suggest, an alternative sense of grace, a more free and democratic sense of motion, than that embodied in the ballet of her time. That's all I meant to say about her.

Primitivism, Modernism, and Dance Theory

Presented by
Marshall Cohen

> "What a charming amusement for your people this is,
> Mr. Darcy!—There is nothing like dancing after all.
> —I consider it one of the first refinements of polished societies."
> "Certainly, Sir;—and it has the advantage also of
> being in vogue amongst the less polished societies
> of the world.—Every savage can dance."
>
> *Pride and Prejudice*

THE THEORY OF MODERN ART tends toward two sharply contrasting ideals. One, deriving from Lessing's *Laocoon*, insists that each art maintain a proper relation to the medium in which it works. This view often incorporates some version of what may be called the principle of modernism in the arts. According to this principle the most advanced, the most significant, the most self-critically modern, or simply the most valuable, works of art are those that do not dissemble the artistic medium in which they are created, or do not trespass on the domain of other artistic media. In one of its forms the doctrine requires that modernist art confine itself to exploiting or to exhibiting only those properties that are essential to a work in the medium it employs. Sometimes, of course, no special value is attached to works which satisfy the modernist ideal. To describe a work as modernist in that case may simply be a way of referring it to a certain style.

The other ideal, which received its most celebrated formulation in Wagner's notion of the *Gesamtkunstwerk*, looks to an art that will draw on the most potent resources of all the major artistic media. This second ideal is often associated with some form of primitivism. A synthesis of the arts is desirable because, only where it is achieved, can we restore that unity of experience and idea, or re-establish that fusion of image and reality, which characterizes primitive art. To be sure, the ideal of the "total work of art" may rest on other than primitivist foundations—a synthesis of the arts may be desired not because it restores some primitive unity but rather because it manifests a transcendental one, or simply because it is supposed to produce singularly powerful sensory effects (to be "cruel"). And it may, of course, be thought that the usable residue of primitive experience can be recaptured within the confines of discrete artistic media. When this approach is taken it is the art of dance that is most often thought to possess a privileged access to the primitive.

At the present time, the modernist ideals of honesty to materials, purification of the medium and even of artistic minimalism prevail and some of the prestige of the most gifted artists derives from the belief that their art adheres to these principles. Merce Cunningham's modernism may appear to provide a counter-example to these observations, for he deploys the arts of language, music and sculpture in his work and collaborates with other artists in a way that is unprecedented since the Diaghilev era. His ideal is, nevertheless, firmly anti-Wagnerian, for, like Brecht, he insists on the integrity of the individual arts and rejects the ideal of fusion. Typically, in his works, the various arts are simply juxtaposed and they proceed in relative independence of one another. Indeed, as Roger Copeland has observed, Cunningham's dancers do not perform *to* music. Rather, they are required to concentrate in such a way as not to be affected by it.[1] (This emphasis on the intellectuality of the dancer is, in fact, a central feature of Cunningham's own reaction against the primitivist tendencies of classical modern dance.) Some of Cunningham's followers pursue a more orthodox approach to the ideals of modernism. They insist that, since dance is created in the medium of the human body, dance should confine itself to examining and revealing the qualities of human movement in greater isolation, for its own sake, and often as it is exhibited in the most ordinary, least dance-like "tasks." More importantly, for present purposes, George Balanchine's admirers have attempted to present him as an artist who has successfully freed dance from its dependence on dramatic representation and theatrical *mise-en-scène*. Abstract possibilities that Marius Petipa adumbrated in, say, *Raymonda*, Act III and *La Bayadère*, Act IV have been pursued and realized with exemplary brilliance in the most advanced modernist works of Balanchine. In these works, *Symphony in C, Agon, Episodes, Stravinsky Violin Concerto*, the essence of the art of ballet stands revealed.

It has not always been so. Frank Kermode, writing as recently as the early Sixties, remarked that during the last sixty or seventy years the peculiar prestige of dance had much to do with "the notion that it somehow represents art in an undissociated and unspecialized form—a notion made explicit by W.B. Yeats and hinted at by Paul Valéry."[2] And Richard Wagner thought the music-drama would, by restoring the undifferentiated unity of the Greek tragic drama, achieve precisely this result. Others looked to something more primitive than Greek tragic drama and were prepared to find a reunification of the arts in places other than Bayreuth. Unquestionably, views such as these influenced the symbolists' reception of Loie Fuller, and prepared the triumph of the Ballets Russes in Paris in 1909. The idea that an integration of the arts is best met in ballet is influential as late as the mid-Thirties. Adrian Stokes, speaking for a significant body of opinion, observed, "Dramatic action or movement and music have consistently inspired the one the other in modern Russian ballet alone. In grand opera, however reformed, they inspire each other at one moment and handicap at the next. Where the work of a Gluck or a Wagner was incomplete, the work of Diaghilev is complete."[3] But it is not ballet alone that is viewed from this kind of perspective. Eric Bentley writes, for instance, that in Graham we find the fullest realization of the magical theater of which Gordon Craig and W.B. Yeats and so many others dreamed.[4]

And Antonin Artaud glimpsed his ideal of total theater, embodied in a "language before speech," in the work of the Balinese theater, which he described as "a kind of superior dance."[5]

This complex of ideas is not, I think, persuasive. Even if we found the ideal of the *Gesamtkunstwerk* more compelling than we do, we would have to acknowledge the crucial fact that the art of dance does not, in general, employ the arts of speech. This is one reason why cinema and some extensions of traditional theater have, more often and more reasonably, been looked to for plausible realizations of the ideal of the *Gesamtkunstwerk*.[6] To be sure, dance could satisfy this requirement by incorporating sung or spoken language as it has in Diaghilev's *Les Noces* and in Martha Graham's *Letter to the World*. But even the success of these works has not pointed the art of dance—or even Diaghilev's or Graham's conceptions of it—in the direction of total theater. It might, of course, be argued that the arts of speech need not be included in a grand synthesis of the arts. This paradox might be argued for by primitivists (and some symbolists) on the ground that dance's non-verbal language of gesture can express meanings and ideas with greater force, precision and economy than is possible for abstract "verbal" languages. Ideas of this sort are unquestionably reflected in Artaud's search for a non-verbal theater and in Mallarmé's observation that the ballerina is not dancing but writing with her body.[7]

But the undifferentiated unity of the primitive world (like the very existence of an emblematic or a transcendental one, which does equivalent work in some related theories) is itself a myth—and a modern one. Even if primitive mysteries are re-enacted, they are experienced by dissociated modern sensibilities and, as some say, only as an aesthetic phenomenon. The art of dance as we know and experience it is one among the arts. It does not displace or incorporate all the other arts, not even all the other theatrical arts. Certainly, the claim that Diaghilev realized the Wagnerian ideal is extravagant and misleading and Diaghilev's contribution does not, in any case, seem as decisive for the aesthetics of dance as it once did. Little of his repertory remains of value. *Parade,* for whose special combination of the arts Guillaume Apollinaire coined the term "surrealism," is sometimes invoked as a brilliant synthesis of the arts. But for Jean Cocteau and his collaborators *Parade* was by design an anti-Wagnerian statement and a repudiation of the "primitivism" of the earlier Diaghilev repertory. In any case, Leonide Massine's choreographic contribution compares unfavorably with the contributions of Cocteau, Picasso and Satie and the work remains unsatisfactory from any point of view.[8] This is not to say there is nothing of value in the Diaghilev inheritance, but what there is certainly does not confirm the view that Diaghilev is complete where Wagner is incomplete. *Petrouchka* is certainly an impressive work (though not the fully-realized masterpiece Stokes and legend suggest) and, like some of the finer works of Graham, it permits dramatic representation and even outright storytelling.[9] In this respect such works unquestionably resist a certain kind of purism, but this is far from showing that they aspire to, or achieve, a full Wagnerian synthesis. In fact, the most fruitful portion of Diaghilev's legacy, works like *Les Sylphides*, parts of *Firebird*, and *Apollo* point in the direction of Balanchine's achievement. Balanchine's art, at its most characteristic, does indeed lean toward the purist ideal. In its most original moments it rejects or attenuates storytelling (though not dramatic implication and metaphor) and derives its imagery mainly from the music to which it is set. But this commitment to music in fact provides an insurmountable obstacle to those who would represent his art, the greatest realization of the art of dance we know, as an embodiment of the purist ideal. For the purist ideal requires the independence (if not necessarily the isolation) of music and drama (they work in two different physical media and are by nature two separate arts). I would not deny, of course, that dance can exist independently of music. Doris Humphrey's *Water Study* and Jerome Robbins's *Moves* show that dances of this sort can achieve remarkable success. We have not been persuaded, however, that dances of this sort represent the ideal realization of the art of dance. Neither primitivism nor modernism in the formulations with which we are most familiar provides an accurate account of dance as we have inherited it or as we prefer it.

In what follows I do not pretend to offer anything like a full discussion of the theory or practice of primitivism or modernism. Given the many possible forms in which these ideas have been or could be developed, any such account in the present compass is out of the question. I do, however, offer a reasonably full discussion of what are perhaps the two most elaborate philosophical discussions of dance to appear in English in recent years, and these essays are usefully read against the background I have sketched. Susanne Langer is by no means the unqualified primitivist some (like Frank

Kermode) have taken her to be, and David Levin (unlike those who inspire him) is not a dogmatic proponent of modernist ideals. Yet primitivist ideas seem to have misled Mrs. Langer as modernist ones have misled David Levin. It is a matter of some interest, I think, that their versions of primitivism and modernism—these two conflicting but intimately related modern artistic options—have led both of them to very similar misinterpretations of the dance as we know it. A criticism of their views should, I believe, contribute to an assessment of the larger body of ideas with which they are associated. And an assessment of modernism and primitivism is, I believe, a central task of contemporary aesthetic theory. T.S. Eliot wrote, "Anyone who would contribute to our imagination of what ballet may perform in (the) future . . . should begin by a close study of dancing among primitive peoples . . ."[10] We have seen that many of the prophets of the *Gesamtkunstwerk* looked into the distant and even into primitive past for a vision of the artwork of the future. Susanne Langer, in the relevant chapters of *Feeling and Form*, goes further. She thinks we must look to primitive dance for an understanding of dance quite generally. Unlike some proponents of the ideal of total theater, however, she does not hope to recover the primitive experience of dance and is therefore not drawn to the theory of the *Gesamtkunstwerk* as a vehicle of that recovery. Indeed, contrary to Frank Kermode's suggestion, she supposes we can only understand the modern art of dance if we understand that the art of dance functions for us in a manner very different from the way it functions in primitive life.[11] Nevertheless, we shall see the idea of the primitive misleads Mrs. Langer, as it has misled the proponents of the ideal of the *Gesamtkunstwerk*, although in a different way.

Mrs. Langer locates the origins of dance in the primitive. Indeed, in her view, it is the first art and "the most serious intellectual business of savage life: it is the envisagement of a world beyond the spot and the moment of one's animal existence, the first conception of life as a whole—continuous, superpersonal life, punctuated by birth and death, surrounded and fed by the rest of nature." But to the "mythic consciousness" these creations are "realities, not symbols. They are not felt to be created by the dance at all, but to be invoked, abjured, challenged, placated, as the case may be. The symbol of the world, the balletic realm of forces, is the world, and dancing is the human spirit's participation in it."[12] But Langer does not suppose the present role of dance is to reconstitute the religious and magical properties primitive dance possessed. Rather, she aligns herself with the tradition of Kant and Schopenhauer and insists that, in order to become an object of aesthetic experience, dance must disengage itself from precisely those practical and cognitive—that is, from those non-aesthetic functions—that it served in primitive life. For Langer, the artist guarantees we can take an aesthetic attitude toward a work of art by creating an object of a special sort, a "virtual" object, or an appearance or illusion, that by its very nature can support only an aesthetic and not a practical interest. In her view, from the physical materials available to an art, the art creates its "primary" illusion. As the painter creates the illusion of space from pigments and canvas, the dancer, working with movements of the human body, creates "a world of powers, made visible by the unbroken fabric of gesture." But an art can never be identified with the materials from which it is made—for these untransformed materials are not, themselves, the pure appearances or semblances or illusions that alone constitute art, and that are alone the proper objects of aesthetic interest. The aesthetic, as opposed to the mythic consciousness, recognizes these illusions for what they are, and does not take the world of illusory Powers to be a reality. The aesthetic object is, by nature, purely visual.

Critics (the present writer included) have elsewhere objected to Langer's notion of illusion or "virtual" object, and questioned whether it is necessary to suppose each art creates objects of this kind to serve as the target of the aesthetic attitude.[13] But it is worth protesting here against the negative view that nothing which can be characterized in purely physical terms (namely, bodily movements) can constitute a work of art, as well as against the positive view that dance is, in fact, an art of illusory gestures. Langer supposes that real gestures are expressions of emotion. She thinks, correctly, that dance theorists (especially theorists of modern dance) have often falsely supposed dances are really expressions of the dancer's (or of the choreographer's) emotions. But she wrongly supposes the proper way to correct this mistake is to declare these expressions of emotion only apparent or illusory. No doubt, this solution appeals to her because, in her view, dance like every other art must present some illusion or other. Why not suppose, then, that dance creates, if not the reality, then the illusion that emotion is being expressed? Mrs. Langer is undoubtedly correct in thinking dancers do not always express emotions, but it is important to insist that they do not always give the impression of expressing them either. Mrs. Langer has merely sophisticated and attenuated the expression theory of dance. She ought to have rejected it outright.

André Levinson long ago remarked on the confusion of gesture with *le pas*. [14] The Rose Adagio or the Act II *pas de deux* in *Swan Lake* may appear to express Aurora's or Odette's emotion (that is, they may be gestures in Langer's sense) but what emotion does the Bluebird *pas de deux* or the dance of the cygnets express? (To be sure, the dance of the cygnets is designed to relieve emotion.) And, then, what emotions does Merce Cunningham express in *How To Pass, Kick, Fall and Run* or Yvonne Rainer in *The Mind is a Muscle, Part I (Trio A)?* Indeed, the movements of these contemporary dances are specifically designed to purge movement of its emotional valence and, in Langer's terms, to leave the materials of dance untransformed into gestures, or the illusion of gestures, or anything else. No doubt there are certain kinds of dances in which the inability to transform movements into gestures does, indeed, amount to failure (though not necessarily in the failure to create a dance). Performing movements with the unearned suggestion that they are endowed with emotional significance is empty rhetoric, and performing them with the suggestion that they are endowed with symbolic import is portentousness. These are, respectively, the characteristic vices of certain schools of dance ("modern" dance) and of certain chore-ographers (Robbins at his worst, Maurice Béjart almost always). I expect it is because we have witnessed these failures and experienced these vices so often that a taste for non-gestural movement has become very strong. However that may be, there is no doubt dances can be constructed that are not gestural in Langer's sense. In fact, we find dances constructed of movements and actions and even of gestures (like the gesture of warning or of recognition), which, since they need not express or appear to express emotion, would not be gestures in Langer's sense. This is not to deny dances may incorporate gestures in Langer's sense—real ones (Isadora Duncan's?) as well as apparent ones (of the sort we find in representational ballets). There is in any case no reason to accept Langer's residual expressionism, or to suppose that if we concede that dances can be constructed of non-illusory physical materials, we will fail to guard against the possibility that someone will take an impermissible, non-aesthetic interest in them. A more pertinent worry would be that far too many dances constructed of pure movement do not support any kind of interest at all.

Even if we waive these objections to the centrality Mrs. Langer assigns to the role of gesture in dance we shall have to object to her view that the dance necessarily creates a "world image," and a world image of a very specific sort. No doubt, her theory marks an advance on those that would return us to a primitive state of mind in which we believe the world image is a reality in which we participate. Mrs. Langer thinks more plausibly that for us dance merely creates an image of the world, an image to which we respond aesthetically. But, like her residual expressionism, her residual primitivism is unconvincing. For on her view, this world image descends from, and bears the (sometimes faded) lineaments of that original primitive world. In Langer's view the world of dance is a world of "interacting forces" which seem "to move the dance itself," whether that image is taken for a reality as by the mythic mind, or acknowledged to be a romantic world or a world of dreams, as it is by the aestheticizing modern mind. [15] Mrs. Langer's characterization of this world is not sufficiently clear for it to be assessed with confidence. But we can wonder whether Jooss's *The Green Table* or Tudor's *The Echoing of Trumpets* inhabits a world of romance, or whether Graham's willful heroines or the contestants in Balanchine's *Agon* seem to be moved by invisible forces rather than to be self-moving. Mrs. Langer's claim becomes somewhat more precise when she says dance movement creates "the illusion of a conquest of gravity, i.e. freedom from the actual forces that are normally known and felt to control the dancer's body." [16] This contention, central to Langer's view of the dance, is surely questionable. No doubt, this kind of thing is often said of ballet, especially of the Romantic ballet which often invokes a supernatural world of anti-gravitational fairies, sylphs and wilis. Even here, of course, this is not the illusion that is always sought. We are all too aware of the pull of gravity on Hilarion as he is danced into the abyss by the wilis. Even more obviously, it was one of the major objectives of the classical modern dance to acknowledge, and even to insist on, the gravitational pull on the dancer's body. Isadora Duncan, no doubt as part of her largely misconceived polemic against ballet, observed that "all movement on earth is governed by the law of gravitation, by attraction and repulsion, resistance and yielding; it is that which makes the rhythm of dance." [17] Graham's floor work was essential to her dance aesthetic, and the relation to earth was a major theme of Humphrey's. (In *Circular Descent*, for example, "she allowed the body to sink into the restful earth and to halt the endless battle against gravitation, and against all opposition.")[18] And it is central in Mary Wigman, the modern dancer whose genius Mrs. Langer paradoxically seems to admire most. (A typical description reports Wigman "tended to kneel, crouch, crowd; her head was often downcast and her arms were rarely lifted high.") Against all this evidence, why does Mrs. Langer persist in her view? Only, so far as I can see, because of her residual primitivism. The world created by the modern dancer, even if it is no longer believed in, must nevertheless present itself as a world of mysterious and invisible "powers," "a Spirit World," free of all physical determination. Mrs. Langer's commitment to her theory seems to overcome her own taste in dance and even, one must suppose, the evidence of her senses.

Even in the case of ballet, as I have suggested, Mrs. Langer's theory is unacceptable. There are, to be sure, moments and even sustained passages in which we might want to agree that the dancer appears to defy the laws of gravity. A good example might be the Bournonville dancer's *grand jeté en avant en attitude* in which, after a quick thrust upwards of the front leg, the back leg shifts high in attitude to "ride" the jump in the air before the front leg is lowered to land, giving the illusion of suspension in the air for several seconds.[19] But illusions of this kind are not essential to ballet and they do not even have priority among the illusions and images ballet projects. Many of the images are not illusory at all: we simply see the dancer performing the classical *pas* and *enchaînements* composed of them. We admire the dancer's speed, grace and fluidity; these are non-illusory features of the dancer's movements and poses. And even where the aesthetic effect of a ballet does depend on an illusion, it may not depend on the illusion or on the visual qualities of the image alone. Aesthetic pleasure is not simply pleasure in the contemplation of images, and dance is not a purely visual art. Our pleasure in ballet is often, in part, a pleasure in the dancer's virtuosity and this requires that we have reason to believe the image is created in a certain way. Fred Astaire, dancing on the wall and across the ceiling in *Royal Wedding,* creates the illusion of a more extreme violation of the laws of gravity than anything we know in traditional ballet. But since we do not believe Astaire was actually photographed dancing on a wall (we are not so sure in the case of Donald O'Connor's "Make 'em Laugh" in *Singin' in the Rain*) this anti-Bazinian cinematic trick gives us none of the pleasure we derive from "antigravitional" illusions in classical ballet. It was only when *Giselle* substituted *pointes* for flying wires that Romantic ballet became a sublime art.[20]

Ballet is not, then, a purely visual art and its images are not necessarily illusory. Ballets may, in fact, require nothing more than an arrangement of the special array of movements consecrated by this art and its traditions. This sort of point is often insisted upon by modernism, but modernism in many of its manifestations yields doctrines as unacceptable as those associated with primitivism. It is to one such theory that we now turn.

In his important essay on "Balanchine's Formalism," David Levin attempts to account for Balanchine's peculiar genius by assimilating his achievement to the modernist aesthetic.[21] Levin's conception of modernism is derived from Clement Greenberg's influential account. In Greenberg's analysis, however, modernism is identified with a number of distinguishable ideas and it will be useful to separate them out. Sometimes Greenberg asserts that the identifying feature of modernist art is its refusal to dissemble the medium. Modernism does not use art to conceal art, but rather to call attention to it. Modernism in this sense requires "frankness."[22] Unlike the Old Masters Edouard Manet "declares" the surfaces on which he paints, and the Impressionists leave no doubt that the colors they use are made of real paint and come from pots and tubes. Ballets are modernist in this sense when they do not dissemble the movements of the dancer's body (and try to create the illusion that the dancer is really a swan or a bluebird). Modernist ballets would acknowledge that the Swan Queen is really a dancer and that her attempts to free her legs from drops of water are made with *petits battements* as the male bluebird's motions are constructed out of *brisés volés* and *cabrioles* (Langer's non-gestural mere twisting and turning in the air?). But in this sense it is easy to exaggerate the extent to which ballet ever seriously dissembled the medium. Even in the most representational of traditional ballets one is meant to remain aware that roles are danced by dancers whose movements are drawn from the repertory of classical technique. To be sure, in some of Balanchine's storyless ballets there is little dissembling at all. But, to my mind, this is a less radical innovation than it may seem. How crucial, after all, are the dissemblings in *Raymonda*, Act III, and *La Bayadère*, Act IV? Although Levin sometimes invokes this conception of modernism, it is not the one that seems mainly to concern him.

148

Sometimes Greenberg means by modernism not a refusal to dissemble the medium, but a refusal to trespass on the domain of another medium.[23] This is the requirement not of frankness, but of propriety. A painting might, for example, meet the requirement of frankness and freely acknowledge the medium in which it is created. But it might be thought to trespass on the domain of literature by telling a story or, as Greenberg thinks traditional painting did, on the domain of sculpture by creating the illusion of three-dimensional space. In order to meet the requirement of propriety, modernist painting had to eschew creating the illusions of three-dimensional tactility and of weight. Painting had to become purely "optical."[24] It is this feature of opticality that Levin fixes on as the distinctive characteristic of Balanchine's modernism. I shall want to question whether Balanchine's ballets do, in fact, possess this characteristic. But, even if they did, it would not follow that they did so because Balanchine was conforming to the modernist canon of propriety. After all, dancing's claim on the third dimension is at least as strong as sculpture's, there is no plausible reason why propriety requires that dance defer to sculpture and confine itself to the realm of the purely optical. Matters are complicated, if not thrown into a hopeless state of confusion, by Greenberg's announcement that the new "constructivist" sculpture which he admires is, like modernist painting, itself essentially optical. But he admits that insofar as this is so "the prohibition on one art's entering the domain of another is suspended."[25] If modernist ballet is to espouse the ideal of "opticality," the canon of propriety will have to be suspended for it as well, and for the same reason. Plainly, the operative theory here is not that each art must confine itself to its distinctive domain, but rather that sculpture and dancing must investigate further the nature of that "opticality" which painting, the avant-garde modernist art, first pursued. But this is a very different demand from the demand for propriety. Its theoretical foundations are obscure, its credentials in modernist theory dubious and its applicability to ballet, even to Balanchine's ballet, implausible. Something like it may be true of the "two-dimensional" effects Nijinsky sought in *Afternoon of a Faun*. But this is a very special case and it certainly does not provide a paradigm of Balanchine's practice.

A third characterization of modernism brings us closer to the main body of Levin's essay. Sometimes Greenberg identifies modernism with the requirement of neither frankness nor propriety (modernism's transformation of the *genre* theorist's decorum) but with what we may call minimalism.[26] This version of modernism excludes, in addition to everything that falls into the domain of another art, everything that is inessential to the art in question. According to minimalism, each art must confine itself to exhibiting its own essential qualities. Modernism in this sense requires that the work of art "reveal," or "make present," the defining conditions for a work of its kind, that is to say, the minimal conditions for being a work in that medium. In what follows we shall identify modernism with minimalism in the sense suggested. In order to understand Levin's view of Balanchine's modernism it will be useful to quote the passage from Levin's essay in which he shows how Greenberg's younger colleague, Michael Fried, applies this modernist doctrine to painting. This will provide the key to Levin's own doctrine of modernist dance. "On Fried's view" he writes, "the two ineluctable defining conditions of painting are its flatness and its shape. No painting can conceivably exist unless it is reduced to flatness and has assumed a certain shape. But since material objects are also shaped and may also be flat, painting can defeat, or suspend, its own objecthood if—and only if—it accomplishes what no mere subject can possibly do: it must somehow materially acknowledge these conditions, rendering them totally present."[27] By revealing this "contradiction" the object establishes its claim to be a work of art.

We may now consider what I take to be Levin's application of this argument to the case of dance. (Some improvisation is necessary, as Levin is not explicit at every point.) The minimal defining condition for dancing is a configuration of physical movements. But, since inanimate objects are also capable of physical movements, dancing must defeat, or suspend, its own physicality and it can do this if—and only if—it accomplishes what no inanimate movement can accomplish: it must somehow acknowledge its own physicality and render it totally present. Modernist dance accomplishes this task by acknowledging the tangible weight and mass of the body but only in order to defeat them, to render the objective body as a magically weightless, optically intangible, presence. In this way the work of art is shown to be a material object and at the same time the "negation" of that objecthood. In order to achieve this suspension of objecthood the dancer's space must be cleared of everything that would locate dance within the binding coordinates of the horizontal field. The failure to do so would prevent the unearthly suspension of objecthood and the possibility of a vertical release into "the sky of grace." It is to help in achieving this minimalist illusion of pure opticality and weightlessness (and now, not to achieve frankness or to maintain propriety, though, given an appropriate understanding of minimalism, they may follow of necessity) that the semantic allusiveness and mimetic gestures of traditional ballet are repudiated in favor of a purely abstract, syntactic symbolism, and that the architectural field of space, traditionally staked out with objects and other dancer's bodies and inflected with color and costume, is avoided. For mimesis and architecture tie the dancer to the horizontal field of beauty and prevent the dancer's vertical release into the realm of the sublime. Something very like the freedom from gravity that for Langer has characterized dance from primitive times and that she associates with its invocation of a world of spirits is viewed by Levin as the minimalist essence of the most advanced modernist art, an art whose essence requires a return to "the sky of God." Unfortunately, I do not believe anything like this view is true, even when it is radically restricted as it is with Levin to the single case of Balanchine's art.

I shall not, here, attempt to criticize Levin's philosophical assumptions in any detail, although the question must at least be raised why the exhibition of movements which present themselves as distinctively human should be sufficient to create ballet or why the intentionality that for Levin characterizes human movement should reveal itself in the illusion of weightlessness or of optically intangible presence. After all, Greenberg finds precisely these qualities in modernist paintings and sculptures. Why, then, can they not be engendered by the movements of non-human, or even by the movements of inanimate, bodies (mobiles)? We shall confine ourselves here, however, simply to questioning whether Balanchine's art, even in its purest examples, is in fact endowed, and uniquely endowed, with the qualities Levin discerns.

It is certainly true that Balanchine tends to avoid storytelling—though even in such central "modernist" works as *Apollo* storytelling is crucial. But it is far from true that he avoids mimetic gesture or dramatic implication. Perhaps his most ubiquitous form of mimesis is found in the imitations and transformations of historical forms of dance—*Agon, Liebeslieder Waltzer, Stars and Stripes, Who Cares?* and *Square Dance* among others. And it has often been remarked that his *pas de deux* constitute an elaborate examination of the relations between the sexes, presenting us with a highly distinctive view of women.[28] This is hardly accomplished by the exclusion of mimetic gesture. Then, too, Balanchine's allusion to the types of human temperament, to the destiny of individuals, to human isolation, triumph and apotheosis, cannot be and has not been missed.[29] If Balanchine makes little use of scenery it is certainly untrue that he refuses to relate dancers to one another in a space that seems corporeally accessible. A major characteristic of Balanchine's choreography is the lucid articulation of physical space—often by great Petipa-like diagonals or by the positioning of discrete groups of dancers against whose locations the trajectory of other dancers is traced or from whose configurations smaller groups of dancers emerge (his familiar "daisy chains, London bridges and turnstile formations").[30] Often the effect of this organization is precisely to bind the dancer to what Levin calls the horizontal space of the stage that the dancer characteristically assaults with his brilliant attack and devours with his speed.

Indeed, it is the speed and physical presence of the Balanchine dancer, rather than her weightlessness (or the tensions generated by that weightlessness) that has usually impressed Balanchine's commentators. It would perhaps be frivolous, though I think it is significant, to mention that Balanchine found a place in his company for Gloria Govrin, who gave the illusion that she was about to ascend into the sky of God no more than the earthbound figures of *Ivesiana* do. If these examples are thought to be eccentric, no one can, I think, make such an objection to Arlene Croce's observation (offered without philosophical *parti pris*) that in the third statement of the theme in *The Four Temperaments* the weight on the dancer's one supporting *pointe* "looks crushing."[31] I do not want to suggest that crushing weight is a quality Balanchine favors, but neither is the quality of weightless opticality on which Levin himself puts such (crushing) weight.

To these observations Levin would reply it is not his view that the dancer simply creates the illusion of weightlessness or of pure opticality. Rather, the dances create a "tense simultaneity" of weight and weightlessness. He points in one place to the Balanchine *plié* in which, despite the dancer's obvious objective weight and effort, Balanchine makes present "at first only in the tensed mode of suppressed virtuality, the graceful arc of flight, which is about to suspend the force of gravity . . ."[32] Quite aside from the doubts one may harbor about whether the dancer in the "arc of flight" actually appears weightless, it is necessary to ask the following questions: are the characteristics here cited really specific to the Balanchine *plié,* or do they not characterize the Bournonville *plié* equally well? And are they in fact characteristic of the Balanchine *plié?* We should remind ourselves that the third girl in *The Four Temperaments,* turned in deep *plié* with the other foot held in *passé* position, reminded Croce of "the bass fiddle the Forties jazz player spins after a chorus of hot licks."[33] Even if we were to accept Levin's description of the Balanchine *plié,* why should we single out this particular moment to carry so heavy a philosophical burden? By what criterion does Levin single it out, or is this a case of selective vision with Heidegger and Clement Greenberg serving as the main selectors? Again, Levin asks us to consider the situation in which the dancer moves dramatically from second position in *demi-plié* (a disposition of the body that forcefully reveals its weight, its objecthood) into a wondrous turn that seems to suspend this condition.[34] In this case we must observe, in the first place, that the alleged impressions of weight and weightlessness are not simultaneous but successive. More important, perhaps, is the fact that even if the wondrous turn is thought to create the impression of weightlessness it certainly does not create the impression of "pictorial flatness" or of "pure opticality." (Roger Copeland has remarked to me that in actual practice the illusion of weightlessness almost invariably induces a kinetic and tactile response in the perceiver that interferes with a purely "optical" appreciation.) Balanchine's dancers are, significantly, turners more than they are jumpers, and these turns establish and insist on the dancer's plasticity, on the fact that the dancer occupies three dimensions. So, too, many of Balanchine's characteristic formations emphasize the three-dimensionality of the dancer. The three muses are posed in arabesque around Apollo and the ballerina's leg, lifted high in attitude, hooks her partner's neck and head in the *Agon pas de deux.* Even Lincoln Kirstein with his talk of "the aria of the aerial"[35] observes that in Balanchine the dancer's silhouette must not be papery, but solid, read in three dimensions. He traces the standards of plastic legibility and expressiveness that govern ballet to that Renaissance sculptural tradition in which "the principle of *contraposto,* a three-quarter view opposition of limbs" dictates "the placement of members as an active spiral, denying any flattening symmetrical frontality."[36] Unquestionably the ideals of Giovanni da

Bologna and Jean Goujon have been modified and to some extent displaced by subsequent cultural and artistic developments. But Balanchine is still to be understood in relation to this tradition and not as a balletic equivalent of David Smith and contemporary constructivism.

As I see it, then, Balanchine does not create the dance equivalent of the purely optical illusions of certain types of modernist painting and sculpture. Rather, Balanchine perpetuates classical ballet's idealization of the human body, though he idealizes it in a specialized, perhaps as many have suggested in a specifically Americanized, way. (It must be admitted, of course, that one man's Americanization is another man's dehumanization.) Indeed, it is reasonable to speculate that a large part of the great popularity film, photography and dance enjoy at the present time derives from the fact that these arts have not "suspended" the objecthood of the human body, or treated it as part of a purely "abstract syntax."[37] Even if Levin were more nearly accurate in his description of Balanchine's dances than I think he is, his interpretation of Balanchine as a minimalizing modernist would be wholly unacceptable for another reason suggested earlier on. The essence of Balanchine is the setting of dances to music. The look of a Balanchine ballet can never be considered in abstraction from the music to which it is set and no consideration of the look of a Balanchine ballet could in itself account for the power of Balanchine's art. Balanchine's dancers do not create the illusion that they are free from the force of gravity; rather they give the impression that their movements are determined by, and reveal the structure of, the music to which they are danced.

Neither the doctrines generated by primitivist commitments nor those elaborated in response to modernist ideals provides an adequate account of the central manifestations and achievements of dance as we know it. Still less, can the character of that art be discovered by considering the nature and possibilities of any particular physical medium, or by imagining how a combination of all the major arts would look. If some of the prestige of twentieth-century dance derives from the assumption that it satisfies one or another of these ideals, its achievements are great enough to survive a more accurate description of its formal nature and its historical qualities. The immensely difficult task of accurate description and adequate theorizing largely remains to be done.

I am grateful to Roger Copeland, Douglas Lackey, Susana Leval and David Levin for helpful comments—M.C.

NOTES

1. Roger Copeland: "The Politics of Perception," *The New Republic* (November 17, 1979), p. 28.
2. Frank Kermode: "Poet and Dancer Before Diaghilev," in *Puzzles and Epiphanies* (London: Routledge and Kegan Paul, 1962), p. 2.
3. Adrian Stokes: *Russian Ballets* (London: Faber and Faber, 1935), p. 114.
4. Eric Bentley: *In Search of Theater* (New York: Vintage Books, 1959), p. 58.
5. Antonin Artaud: *The Theater and Its Double* (New York: Grove Press, 1958), p. 58.
6. Susan Sontag: "Film and Theater" reprinted in Mast, Gerald and Marshall Cohen (eds.), *Film Theory and Criticism,* second ed. (New York: Oxford University Press, 1979), p. 375.
7. Bradford Cook (tr.): *Mallarmé: Selected Prose Poems, Essays and Letters* (Baltimore: The Johns Hopkins Press, 1956), p. 62.
8. E.T. Kirby (ed.): *Total Theater: A Critical Anthology* (New York: E.P. Dutton and Co., 1969), p. xxiv.
9. David Vaughan: "Fokine in the Contemporary Repertory," *Ballet Review 7,* nos. 2 and 3 (1978-79), p. 22.
10. T.S. Eliot: quoted in Kermode, op. cit., p. 3.
11. Ibid., p. 2.
12. Susanne K. Langer: *Feeling and Form* (New York: Charles Scribner and Sons, 1953), p. 190.
13. Marshall Cohen: "Appearance and The Aesthetic Attitude," *The Journal of Philosophy LVI,* no. 23 (November 5, 1959), pp. 921-924. Samuel Bufford, "Langer Evaluated: Susanne Langer's Two Philosophies of Art," Reprinted in Dickie, George and Richard Sclafani (eds.), *Aesthetics, A Critical Anthology* (New York: St. Martin's Press, 1977), pp. 168-178.
14. André Levinson: "The Idea of the Dance, From Aristotle to Mallarmé," *Theater Arts Monthly,* (August 1927), p. 576.
15. Langer, op cit., p. 201.
16. Ibid., p. 194.
17. Walter Terry: *The Dance in America,* rev. ed. (New York: Harper and Row, 1971), p. 43.
18. Ibid., p. 108.
19. Henry Haslam: "How to Perform Bournonville," *Ballet Review 2,* no. 6, p. 23.
20. Peggy Van Praagh and Peter Brinson: *The Choreographic Art* (New York: Alfred A. Knopf, 1963), p. 33.
21. David Michael Levin: "Balanchine's Formalism," *Dance Perspectives 55* (Autumn 1973), pp. 29-48. Reprinted in *Salmagundi,* special issue on *Dance* (Spring-Summer 1976), pp. 216-236.
22. Clement Greenberg: "Modernist Painting," in Gregory Battcock: *The New Art: a critical anthology* (New York: E.P. Dutton, 1966), p. 163.

23. Clement Greenberg: "The New Sculpture," *Art and Culture* (Boston: Beacon Press, 1961), p. 139.
24. Ibid., p. 144.
25. Ibid., p. 143.
26. Clement Greenberg: "After Abstract Expressionism," *Art International VI* (October, 1962), p. 29. For a fuller discussion of Greenberg's views see my "Notes on Modernist Art," *New Literary History III* (1971-2), pp. 220-223.
27. Levin, op. cit., p. 33.
28. Arlene Croce: *Afterimages* (New York: Alfred A. Knopf, 1977), p. 127. My obligations to this work go well beyond the footnotes I have supplied.
29. Ibid., pp. 185-190.
30. Roger Copeland: "Balanchine—Ballet's First Modernist," *The New York Times (Arts and Leisure)*, January 15, 1978.
31. Croce, op. cit., p. 188.
32. Levin, op. cit., p. 42.
33. Croce, op. cit., p. 188.
34. Levin, op. cit., p. 46.
35. Lincoln Kirstein: "Classic Ballet: Aria of the Aerial," *Playbill* (New York: American Theater Press, Inc., May 1976), pp. 3ff.
36. Lincoln Kirstein: *"The Classic Ballet: Basic Technique and Terminology"* (New York: Alfred A. Knopf, 1977), p. 5.
37. Roger Copeland: "Photography and The World's Body," *The Massachusetts Review* (Winter, 1978), pp. 797ff.

DISCUSSION FOLLOWING
MARSHALL COHEN PRESENTATION

Panelists: Anna Kisselgoff, Gerald Myers, Laura Dean, Thomas Wartenberg, Marshall Cohen

ANNA KISSELGOFF: I happen to agree with most of what Marshall says. I'm particularly interested in the Balanchine question, because I think what Levin said in his essay was really said thirty years before by John Martin in one of his lectures at the New School. He was defining modern dance. And, of course, his most famous statement was that "modern dance is not a system; it is a point of view." His unhappiness with ballet at the time in the Thirties was that it was really unable to find its modernist ideal in the way he felt modernism was being defined in the Thirties. And it's wrong to think Martha Graham was old hat and a Romantic at that time. Certainly she was being compared to Picasso and the Cubists, and certainly *Primitive Mysteries* is formally as stark a work as you can get, and it has survived today. That isn't so because we're concerned about a neo-Indian ritual from the Southwest of somebody's imagination. It's because we are really concerned with the patterns as they exist on stage.

Keep in mind there was no American ballet tradition when Martin was writing, no native ballet tradition, and all he had been seeing was the Ballet Russe as brought over by Sol Hurok, and he was very unhappy with it. But he predicted the real course Balanchine's work has taken, which it had not taken at that time. Keep in mind the first totally plotless ballet Balanchine ever did was in 1941, *Concerto Barocco. Serenade* is really more a direct outgrowth of the work he had seen in the Soviet Union in the Twenties. So what I felt was the key statement Martin made is that ballet can find its modernism only when it recognizes the autonomy of its technique—in other words, when the form and the content are fused. I find the medium of ballet is not necessarily the physical human body, but the academic language. And I stress the word "language" because people have always said to me that ballet is so tradition-minded. Well, the tradition is in the training. The tradition is not onstage. You can use ballet as a language to do things, as Levin suggests, that square with the modernist ideal. You can put on Chinese revolutionary ballets and propaganda ballets, and you can put on spectacles. John Martin was saying that when ballet realizes it should concentrate on its essence, which is the idiom itself, then he felt it would find a more contemporary and more modernist solution. That essence was being camouflaged by the spectacle of the Massine productions, which was what Martin was seeing at that time.

GERALD MYERS: Laura, do you think you're trying essentially to create illusions on the stage?

LAURA DEAN: Well, I think in any art form it's another way of talking. Language is one way of talking, and whether you're painting or making a dance or making a piece of music or making an apple pie, or whatever you're doing, I think it's a way of talking and you're expressing something. And it's in the nature of the performing arts that when you are gaining a certain kind of attention from a spectator, you are creating an illusion.

MYERS: I read something about your concept of choreography,

and as I watched you in your new piece, I thought I could see your concern with geometrical figures and patterns and with infusing those with a certain kind of energy. I want to try this out on you and ask you: do you think you're moving in circles and spinning, or are you really getting patterns and circles to move themselves?

DEAN: That's nice and poetic. I think it's very nice. I would say yes to both.

MYERS: I feel like a winner.

TOM WARTENBERG: I think one of the difficulties we have to overcome here is that philosophers seem to speak a different language from that of dancers. But basically, it seemed to me what Marshall was trying to say, or one of the important parts was that there are different ideals people have thought dance ought to be instantiating. One of the things I wanted to ask is what the status of these ideals is supposed to be. The Wagnerian, the purified minimalist, and then later, this Balanchine notion of a mixture of dance and music, I gather, are the three basic ideals dance has been or could approximate. One of the interesting things for me was thinking about Laura's dances and wondering if she thinks they approach one ideal rather than another. I won't say what I think, but I'd like to hear what she has to say about that. But I was wondering what these ideals are supposed to be. What status does Marshall think they have? You see, one of the things that seems to me most suspicious about aestheticians is that they tend to specify ideals that dance or art ought to correspond to, but art always seems to go ways that aestheticians don't understand. For one thing, it seems to me difficult to justify what sort of an ideal an art form ought to move towards, because I'm not sure how one would go about doing that, since it presupposes you understand the nature of the materials of the art form and that's one of the questions you're trying to answer by specifying the ideals. These ideals, it seems to me, can't really function as norms very well, and I'd like to know, then, exactly what they're supposed to be doing. And, again, one of the things, it seems to me, about artists, is that they change our understanding of the medium itself. I think people like Picasso and Martha Graham change our understanding of what the medium was, so, in a certain way, philosophers always come to the scene a little late. Perhaps a better way of thinking about these ideals—and I'm not sure if this is what Marshall meant—is that they explain to us what dance is, where the power of dance arises. That is, these are different sorts of groupings under which we can lump dances together, and by which we are able to articulate our preferences. By the way, I assume that at some level Laura's dances are much more like this Wagnerian ideal.

One of the other things I wanted to talk about is this notion of weightlessness, which a number of critics and philosophers seem to think is very important about dance. I think, as it's stated literally, it's absurd. I mean, you don't want to see dancers rising like helium balloons and demonstrating weightlessness to you. On the other hand, I think Marshall said, what's really behind this notion of weightlessness is that there is a certain idealization of human physicality underlying a lot of dance. This idealization is, I think, one that ought to convey a certain amount of effortlessness rather than weightlessness. That is, most of what dancers do takes a lot of energy, but when you are watching them they don't convey "effort" to you. I mean, they don't grunt and groan all the time when they're doing things that are hard. They're concealing from you a lot of the physical effort that goes into their movements. I was thinking about this just now, and I thought in a certain sense there's a connection between willing something and execution in dance that's quite different from what most of us do. We are comparatively clumsy and we're hampered by our physicality much more than dancers are, and I think dance tries to convey this sort of effortlessness with which the will is instantiated in the physical world.

MYERS: I think Marshall might want to make a response at this time.

MARSHALL COHEN: Let me start with Tom's remarks and say, first of all, he has understood me very well. I began by talking about two contrasting aesthetic ideals, ideals which, I must emphasize, have not been imposed by philosophers. They are ideals that have been articulated and championed by critics and creative artists as well. I think there can be no doubt that sometimes artists or writers do endorse a particular ideal as the proper one, or the most fruitful one. And one thing I wanted to say was that I don't think the great works of art of our time clearly satisfy either of the ideals I sketched, though some of them plainly tend toward one ideal rather than the other. We need to reject the exclusive claims of both of them. If we accepted Langer's theory, we could not account for the existence of minimalist, physicalist works, for they do not transform physical movements into "gestures." I think Langer's theory is unacceptable for this reason. Similarly, I don't think the ideal of the *Gesamtkunstwerk*—an ideal that has been very powerful in certain artistic circles—is especially characteristic of the great works of our century. Although some critics think much of the work of the Diaghilev period conforms to this ideal, I'm skeptical. That's one reason I discussed that period (and Graham, too) and I wondered what Anna thought of the claim I made.

I also had some of these questions in mind in connection with Laura Dean's dance, which I saw for the first time last night and admired very much. Frankly, I wasn't expecting to admire it as much as I did. But it did raise certain questions for me and they were not unrelated to the subject of my talk. One question is this: did it participate, perhaps even consciously, in something like the "Wagnerian" ideal? I heard a number of people in the audience say it was an attempt to provide us with the experience of a ritual, and not simply a work aimed at engendering an aesthetic experience (of the kind Lessing and Langer think characteristic of art as we moderns know it). Was it an attempt to go behind, or beyond, "aesthetic experience," an attempt to recreate religious ritual or primitive magic? People were saying (and they weren't all recent victims of an aesthetics course), "I didn't really have an aesthetic experience; it was more like taking part in a ritual." If these were plausible observations, it would seem Laura Dean tends more toward one of the ideals I was talking about than she does toward the other.

I did have one problem with Laura Dean's dance that was not unconnected to my attempt to discern her intentions. I'm still not sure whether I regard this as a flaw. At one point in the dance each of the dancers executes a series of steps that looked like what in the terminology of classical ballet would be called a *manège* of *tours jetés*. I thought this was a provocative, but unsuccessful, invocation of ballet and I wondered why, in this dance, which seemed not to participate in the ballet idiom, this apparently deliberate invocation of ballet was made. And in thinking about that I had to think about

Laura Dean's intentions, about whether or not she was trying explicitly to distinguish her dance from ballet, or was making a point about ballet, and so on. Even in assessing last night's experience, then, ideas like those I discussed in my talk seemed to obtrude themselves. And it wasn't, as I say, I alone who felt them. I heard many members of the audience address them quite spontaneously after the performance.

But, to get back to what Tom was saying, my general message is one of electicism. We cannot accept the ideas of either Langer or Clement Greenberg as adequate to the variety of twentieth-century art.

DEAN: We're talking about Western dance in the twentieth century?

COHEN: I am. Of course, the view that's hinted at in associating primitivism with the Wagnerian ideal is that one of the features of twentieth-century art has been to affect primitivism and to look to other cultures. Ballet dancers were Antonin Artaud's ideal, and of course in Picasso and in painters of that period we get African sculpture involved and so forth.

DEAN: That's a point I'd like to go into a little further. When we discuss art, we have to realize we are discussing it within certain time periods, and if we want to open it up, we could be talking about, for example, ancient Greek art. Where was that coming from, and is that closer to the Wagnerian ideal? With regard to Langer's concept of the aerial quality in dance, she seems to have excluded more than 80 per cent of the dance that's happened on the face of this earth since its beginnings. Consult any history of dance, such as Sach's *The World History of Dance,* and you will see that most of the dance, if anything, is very much into the ground. All of Eastern dance is very heavily weighted into the ground. So are dances in South America and most folk dances which in actual fact are quite old.

And so the aerial viewpoint in dance is relatively recent in a long history of dance and it's something that came out of the French courts. This aerial point of view is evident again when women began to go up on *pointe.*

Also Marhsll, you use the term "Judson minimalists." I was a little confused about that because I'm not sure whether the word "minimalist" was being used in 1965 or thereabouts.

KISSELGOFF: No, you're right. It was applied afterwards. Certainly they didn't call themselves that.

I do take the exclusivist position. I think one of the reasons Judson reached a dead end was that it was using ideas transposed from the art world, and once they had explored these possibilities, that was it, and many of the Judson people, with very few exceptions, have actually stopped working in dance. I didn't hear the word "minimalist" applied then. I mean, now people talk about "postmodern" and "new dance," but it was just Judson Dance Theater, I think, during the actual time. I should point out here that there has been some confusion about Laura's work, which I do not take to be minimalist, though it has been referred to as such. The confusion occurs because outwardly the vocabulary is reduced and that is confused with minimal.

Marshall, you talked about the ritual aspect, but certainly Judson was not interested in rituals.

COHEN: No, I wasn't suggesting that.

KISSELGOFF: No, but Laura Dean's work certainly creates an effect through the cumulative impact of the kind of movement she's using and the way she's using it, and that doesn't approach in any way the purist ideal you're talking about.

COHEN: I'd like to introduce a distinction that Roger Copeland, whom I see sitting in the audience, has made. There are two different uses that can be made of simple movements in dance. One use concentrates your attention on the actual, physical features of the movement. Another, which I think is more like Laura Dean's use of it, works to induce a certain psychological state. Certainly, that's how a lot of people react to her work, so that, although she employs insistent repetitions and simplified movements, she is far from pursuing what I take to be the ideal of the Judson minimalists, which is closer to the first use I mentioned. Laura, I wasn't thinking of you that way at all. In fact, that's why I'm seconding Tom. I think a lot of people coming to your work with that expectation were surprised to find you more a Wagnerian than a minimalist.

KISSELGOFF: You speak of Laura's "insistent repetitions," but Laura doesn't like the word "repetition." She says she is not repeating.

DEAN: Some people get taken aback with my use of the term "repetition" because they think I am being heavy-handed, but to me it's quite simple. To me, the word "repetition" exists within the physical time-sense, but I don't see it existing within the intelligence. I think there is a difference there, and we get back to that old statement that you can't step into the same river twice. Other than that, I don't fight the word "repetition."

WARTENBURG: While we are on Laura's choreography there is a question I would like to bring up. One of the interesting things about modern dance is that often the same person who's the choreographer also leads the company and dances herself or himself. This seems to be very different from theater, where you have different individuals writing a script, directing it and acting in it. Each viewpoint is filled by a different person, but this is often not the case in modern dance. I would think this would lead to certain problems.

KISSELGOFF: Well, I know Balanchine told me one reason he doesn't hanker after modern dance or cotton to it at all is he finds that when the choreographer is also the main dancer, the choreographer is physically limiting the capacities of the other dancers and then cannot expand the vocabularies and the capacities of the dancers beyond what they can do. His whole idea has been to extend the vocabulary of classical ballet, and that is in fact what he has done. This is why he also prefers to be, as you know, classed as a descendent of Petipa, because he felt Petipa took the vocabulary that had existed before and pushed dancers to what they previously thought they were incapable of doing. He has expanded the language of dance, which was done on stage, not in the classroom. It was done through the creative act. Balanchine uses his dancers as creative instruments. But, he says, when a dancer is required to move in one way, and he named a very popular modern dancer who insists all the dancers in her company must move the way she does, then she is limiting not only their dancing but her own creative possibilities. He said, "I've been very fortunate in that I am not a dancer."

MYERS: Anna, you referred to the expansion of the vocabulary by Balanchine, the ballet vocabulary. I brought you into a discussion in an earlier session, because you were quoted in a recent interview as having said the critic is using a tired language, and the dance critic needs to evolve a new vocabulary.

KISSELGOFF: I do agree with that. I think, as Marshall has said, there has been very little serious criticism. Part of the problem is in the language of the writer, also that dance is a repertory art, and it's a live performing art, and the tendency is to see the same works over and over again, and people fall into routines. If they haven't found the vocabulary, especially to describe a new form of dancing, then they will fall into a rut.

COHEN: It may be that we need a new language of criticism. But in fact we have a perfectly good language, the English language, which critics and philosophers unfortunately vastly abuse. And one of the reasons I wanted to criticize Langer for saying all dance movement is "gesture" is that in ordinary English we would not describe all dance movements as gestures. We distinguish in English between a movement, a gesture, an action, and so on. Now, if the people who wrote about dance would just use English correctly, and observe those distinctions which they constantly obscure, we'd be much better off than we are now. Of course, I don't know what Anna has in mind in calling for a new language of criticism. But one of the mercies of dance criticism is that semiology hasn't taken it over as it has film criticism. That's one possibility. Unfortunately, we've had a certain amount of Jungian and Freudian language introduced into dance criticism. But I myself think though innovative concepts may in certain circumstances be helpful and necessary (as the technical language of classical ballet is), the main problem with dance criticism is, as I've said, that it fails to use, that indeed it abuses, English. I was trying to show, in discussing some influential aesthetic theories, that they can't even be expressed in a fully intelligible way because one often doesn't know whether people are employing concepts like movement or gesture in the normal English sense or in some other, often ill-defined, technical sense.

AUDIENCE: To come back to Susanne Langer—so far as I remember, the quotations are from her chapter "Magic Circle" where she talks about virtual gesture. That means—maybe I'm not correct—she is talking about the magic force of dance, and I don't see any contradiction between what Wigman did and what Laura Dean did because both are interested in ritual, as you say yourself. So to put it on the minimal side seems to me a pretty bad deviation. Did I misunderstand you?

COHEN: I think you misunderstood me a little bit, and Susanne Langer a little bit, too. I think Susanne Langer is not wholly clear about this herself, but for her the basic problem of a philosophy of art is: How does the artist create aesthetic experiences and what are they? And in the tradition deriving from Kant and Schopenhauer and Schiller she contrasts aesthetic experience with practical experience, on the one side, and with religious and mythical experience on the other. She thought dance was the first, the most primitive art, and she thought the problem about dance was, how can that which was *once* myth and ritual become something quite different— aesthetic experience? She didn't, in fact, think Wigman's dances were myth or ritual. Neither did she think they were a form of self-expression, as many people thought. For her they provided an *image* or an *illusion* of self-expression and ritual, not self-expression and ritual themselves. So I don't think your interpretation of what Langer actually thought is quite right.

Now if Laura Dean or some other like-minded artist is saying to us the modern idea of aesthetic experience is a sterile one, and if they are asking why we should limit works of art to creating mere aesthetic experiences as opposed to providing practical experiences, or to invoking the experience of ritual or religion, then they are rejecting this ideal, the ideal of aesthetic experience, which has predominated in philosophical and critical aesthetics in the West for about 200 years now and which Langer very much accepts. If Laura Dean is in fact trying to reconstitute magic or ritual she is doing something

Langer did not accept as a proper objective for art. For Langer it would be a form of cultural regression.